VCAP5-DCD
Official Cert Guide

VMware Press is the official publisher of VMware books and training materials, which provide guidance on the critical topics facing today's technology professionals and students. Enterprises, as well as small- and medium-sized organizations, adopt virtualization as a more agile way of scaling IT to meet business needs. VMware Press provides proven, technically accurate information that will help them meet their goals for customizing, building, and maintaining their virtual environment.

With books, certification and study guides, video training, and learning tools produced by world-class architects and IT experts, VMware Press helps IT professionals master a diverse range of topics on virtualization and cloud computing. It is the official source of reference materials for preparing for the VMware Certified Professional Examination.

VMware Press is also pleased to have localization partners that can publish its products into more than 42 languages, including Chinese (Simplified), Chinese (Traditional), French, German, Greek, Hindi, Japanese, Korean, Polish, Russian, and Spanish.

For more information about VMware Press, visit **vmwarepress.com.**

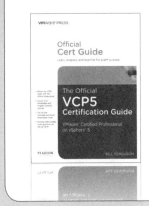

VCAP5-DCD
Official Cert Guide

Paul McSharry

vmware® PRESS

Upper Saddle River, NJ • Boston • Indianapolis • San Francisco
New York • Toronto • Montreal • London • Munich • Paris • Madrid
Capetown • Sydney • Tokyo • Singapore • Mexico City

VCAP5-DCD Official Cert Guide

Published by Pearson plc

Publishing as VMware Press

Library of Congress Control Number: 2013909347

ISBN-13: 978-0-7897-5018-1

ISBN-10:   0-7897-5018-X

Text printed in the United States of America

First Printing August 2013

Warning and Disclaimer

Corporate and Government Sales

VMware Press offers excellent discounts on this book when ordered in quantity for bulk purchases or special sales, which may include electronic versions and/or custom covers and content particular to your business, training goals, marketing focus, and branding interests. For more information, please contact

U.S. Corporate and Government Sales
(800) 382-3419
corpsales@pearsontechgroup.com

For sales outside the United States, please contact:

International Sales
international@pearsoned.com

VMWARE PRESS PROGRAM MANAGERS
Erik Ullanderson
Anand Sundaram

ASSOCIATE PUBLISHER
David Dusthimer

ACQUISITIONS EDITOR
Joan Murray

DEVELOPMENT EDITOR
Ellie Bru

MANAGING EDITOR
Sandra Schroeder

PROJECT EDITOR
Seth Kerney

COPY EDITOR
Kitty Wilson

INDEXER
Larry D. Sweazy

PROOFREADER
Dan Knott

COORDINATOR
Vanessa Evans

BOOK DESIGNER
Chuti Prasertsith

COMPOSITION
Bumpy Design

Contents at a Glance

Table of Contents

About the Author

Paul McSharry is an independent virtualization consultant and instructor based in the UK. He has been an IT professional for 15 years and now specializes in virtualization technologies and web hosting solutions, working with large retail and financial enterprises.

When not working in the field, he is often instructing the VMware-authorized classes for various VMware VATCs.

Paul holds a variety of vendor-based IT certifications, such as MCSE, MCITP, VCP, and VCAP, and he is also a qualified IT instructor, holding VMware Certified Instructor (VCI), CompTIA CTT+, and Microsoft MCT credentials.

His recent consultancy projects include the following:

- Producing a large-scale hybrid cloud platform to deploy and enable secure e-discovery web-based applications for data review

- Several large datacenter migrations using various vSphere platforms

- Multiple public and private vCloud director platform designs and implementations

- Several enterprise-wide VMware view-based VDI deployments

Paul is an active blogger (http://www.elasticsky.co.uk) and Twitter user (@pmcsharry). He has also been awarded the vExpert designation for his work in the VMware community for two years running (2012–2013).

Dedication

For my family—Carolyn, Harrison, and Sadie
xxx

Acknowledgments

The past 18 months or so have been a very busy time; my son, Harrison, made the transition from being a toddler to being a little boy, and my baby daughter, Sadie, arrived. Soon after, my wife and I moved and settled in a different part of the UK. As these life-changing events occurred, I continued to consult and teach using VMware technology.

Writing this book was challenging, not only given my already busy life, but because effectively writing a guide on how to design rather than simply providing information on how a specific product works or creating lab exercises was a bit of a change from anything I have ever tried to do before.

I would like to first thank my children, who had to play without their dad while he was writing this guide.

I would also like to thank the team at Pearson, who were very helpful and patient, to say the least. I'm sure I asked a lot of silly questions.

Thanks also to the team at VMware Education for providing such great reference content in the VCI channel.

Finally, I would like to thank my wife, Carolyn, for all her help and suggestions, and for living with this project. I would not have finished it without her.

About the Reviewers

Manish Patel has more than 14 years of experience as an IT professional, and is currently working at VMware Canada as a senior TSE. He also possesses various industry certifications, including VCP3,4,5-DV/DT/Cloud, VCAP4/5-DCA, VTSP 5, MCSA/E, SCNA, SCSA, CCNA, CNE, CNA, and Compaq ASE. Manish was recently named a vExpert 2013 for his contributions to the VMware community. Readers can visit Manish on LinkedIn at http://ca.linkedin.com/pub/manish-patel/5/249/12b/, where he maintains several groups, including VCAP-DCD, vCloud, View, and VMware Orchestrator, as well as on Twitter (@mandivs).

Tom Ralph is an early adopter and firm believer in VMware technologies, with more than eight years of experience in architecture, optimization, and troubleshooting of complex virtual environments dating back to ESX 2.5. He is an expert in VMware Cloud, network security solutions, and architecture. In addition to holding VCDX (3, 4, and 5) certification, Tom holds VCP (3, 4, and 5), VCAP-DCD 4 and 5, and VCAP-DCA 4. In his current role as an architect with the Cloud Tenant Operational group, he focuses on the creation of service definitions, the consumption of cloud resources, and the definition of consumption methods for cloud infrastructures. In his spare time, he can be found authoring the *Official VCP-Cloud Certification Guide* for VMware Press.

Gabrie van Zanten is a virtualization specialist working for Open Line in the Netherlands. As a consultant, he designs and implements virtual infrastructures for customers. Besides being a consultant, Gabrie runs one of the top-ranked blogs on VMware at www.GabesVirtualWorld.com. He writes about VMware and helps his readers get in-depth understanding on how VMware products work. His blogging activities, the presentations he gives, and the effort he puts into helping members of the VMware community earned him the VMware vExpert award 2009 through 2012.

We Want to Hear from You!

As the reader of this book, *you* are our most important critic and commentator. We value your opinion and want to know what we're doing right, what we could do better, what areas you'd like to see us publish in, and any other words of wisdom you're willing to pass our way.

We welcome your comments. You can email or write us directly to let us know what you did or didn't like about this book—as well as what we can do to make our books better.

Please note that we cannot help you with technical problems related to the topic of this book.

When you write, please be sure to include this book's title and author as well as your name, email address, and phone number. We will carefully review your comments and share them with the author and editors who worked on the book.

Email: VMwarePress@vmware.com

Mail: VMware Press
ATTN: Reader Feedback
800 East 96th Street
Indianapolis, IN 46240 USA

Reader Services

Visit our website and register this book at www.informit.com/title/9780789750181 for convenient access to any updates, downloads, or errata that might be available for this book.

Introduction

Welcome to *VCAP5-DCD Official Cert Guide*. I am extremely honored to be able to present this guide to you in conjunction with VMware Press.

As a full-time consultant working with virtualization every day, I found the writing process challenging. It was extremely useful for me to question not only how to best create a guide to pass the advanced VMware certification but also how to provide you, the reader, some takeaway aspects that could be put into use in the field—which, after all, is the main reason to complete the certification in the first place.

I have worked in the IT industry for 15 years, in both training and consultancy roles. I have tried to add value from my experience, using various real-life examples in the explanations.

This book is designed to help you study for the VCAP5-DCD exam. It is not a definitive guide to designing VMware technology, nor is it a complete reference book for all material in the exam. I have intentionally decided not to try to reinvent or rewrite content already available in the VMware community but to concentrate on the thought processes that an architect should use in design work.

This guide is not only based on real-world projects but also on my experience of passing the VCAP4-DCD and VCAP5-DCD exams while teaching the vSphere design workshops.

I have purposely stripped the content right down to the processes that the VCAP5-DCD blueprint concentrates on and the specific knowledge required by a professional VMware architect. Knowledge of a product is one thing; how to use that information to create a good design is something else entirely.

Who Should Read This Book

This guide is aimed at anyone looking to pass the VCAP5-DCD exam, but also at existing vSphere engineers looking to make the transition from supporting systems to designing platforms. There is a change in skill set in the role transition, and it is often hard to find study material—you are more likely to learn from experience. I have tried to bridge this gap throughout the guide.

Goals and Methods

My number one goal of this book is simple: to help you pass the VCAP5-DCD certification test and obtain the status of VMware Certified Advanced Professional – Data Center Design.

To aid you in gaining the knowledge and understanding of key topics, I use the following methods:

- **Opening topics list:** This list defines the topics to be covered in the chapter. Each chapter is a part of the exam blueprint and the chapters and topics are written in blueprint order.

- **"Do I Know This Already?" quizzes:** At the beginning of each chapter is a quiz. The quizzes, and answers/explanations (found in Appendix A), are meant to gauge your knowledge of the subjects. If the answers to the questions do not come readily to you, be sure to read the entire chapter.

- **Key topics:** The key topics indicate important figures, tables, and lists of information that you should know for the exam. They are interspersed throughout the chapter and are listed in table format at the end of the chapter.

- **Review questions:** All chapters conclude with a set of review questions to help you assess whether you have learned the key material in the chapter.

- **Exam-type questions:** Exam questions are included with the printed and digital editions of this book. They are written to be as close to the type of questions that appear on the VCAP5-DCD exam.

How to Use This Book

The VCAP5-DCD is an advanced-level certification; it requires you to have attained a VCP-level certification and relevant professional real-world experience using the technologies. It is a very different exam from the VCP5-DCV and VCAP5-DCA exams. The VCAP5-DCD exam is based on making informed and pragmatic design choices using VMware platforms.

A designer requires a broad knowledge of all linking technologies and must do extensive reading around the subject. Unfortunately, there are no shortcuts around this!

Due to the amount of material available for VMware technologies, preparing for the VCAP5-DCD exam can be very daunting, and many professionals I have spoken to during courses I have led or in various contract roles have said that they find all the following difficult:

- Understanding where to start with correct platform design

- Knowing what aspects of the technology to cover and to what level of detail

- Knowing when to take the exam

This guide was created with these uncertainties in mind.

I recommend that you use this book as a guide to help you study other material. For each objective in the blueprint I do the following:

- Discuss the important concepts needed for the exam

- Relate real-life examples to the content

- Set tasks that can be used to prepare for the exam

- Recommend further reading to add to your growing knowledgebase

Once you have read all the chapters in this book and have completed the exam preparation tasks, you should have the basis of a real-life designer's toolkit.

This set of documentation and processes can be used for real designs in the field and to study for the VCAP5-DCD exam.

The core chapters of this book, Chapters 1–7, cover the following topics:

- **Chapter 1, "Introduction to Technical Design":** This chapter focuses on the design process and associated terminology.

- **Chapter 2, "Creating a Design":** This chapter focuses on information gathering and logical design presentation.

- **Chapter 3, "Thoughts on Good Choices for Virtualization and Design":** This chapter focuses on the impact of specified and sometimes assumed business expectations on platform design.

- **Chapter 4, "Developing a Design on Paper and Delivering It Physically":** This chapter focuses on creating logical designs and the process to develop them into a physical design.

- **Chapter 5, "Virtual Machine Design":** This chapter focuses on the thoughts and options that can be used to ensure that an appropriate virtual guest is produced for an application workload.

- **Chapter 6, "Project Execution":** This chapter focuses on the order of delivery, task validation, and project documentation.

- **Chapter 7, "Tips for Passing the Exam":** This chapter focuses on final exam tips and strategies, as well as a review of the VCAP5-DCD exam experience.

The Designer's Toolkit

All engineers have a folder or USB stick with a collection of their favorite tools, scripts, and tricks. The purpose of this book is to help you create your own folder for design work.

Your folder should include the following:

- A well-understood design process
- A checklist and process for good design questions
- A high-level design template
- Worked examples of the following:
  - Entity relationship diagrams
  - Logical design diagrams
  - Physical design diagrams
  - A milestone project implementation plan
  - Walkthrough documentation
  - A high-level disaster recovery plan document
  - A virtual machine/workload/vApp design template
- A test/validation plan
- An implementation plan

The VCAP5-DCD certification exam will be updated as the certification is updated. As VMware develops more exciting functionality, the blueprint will also change with respect to technology, but the overall theme of and feeling behind this certification should not. After all, platform design processes and thoughts do not change; the technologies do.

Passing the VCAP5-DCD certification exam will validate your skills in design and translating business requirements into technical requirements and creating suitable technical documentation. These skills are very important, regardless of what technology is used. Therefore, in my opinion, VCAP5-DCD has been the most useful non-defense-based IT certification I have ever completed. I hope you enjoy the study!

The VCAP5-DCD Certification Exam and This Book

Table I-1 maps the VCAP5-DCD exam topics to the chapters of this book that cover them.

Table I-1   VCAP5-DCD Exam Topics and Chapter References

Exam Section/Objective	Chapter Where Covered
Section 1: Plan, Install, Configure, and Upgrade vCenter Server and VMware ESXi	
Objective 1.1 – Install and Configure vCenter Server	Chapter 1
Objective 1.2 – Install and Configure VMware ESXi	Chapter 1
Objective 1.3 – Plan and Perform Upgrades of vCenter Server and VMware ESXi	Chapter 1
Objective 1.4 – Secure vCenter Server and ESXi	Chapter 1
Objective 1.5 – Identify vSphere Architecture and Solutions	Chapter 1
Section 2 – Plan and Configure vSphere Networking	
Objective 2.1 – Configure vNetwork Standard Switches	Chapter 2
Objective 2.2 – Configure vNetwork Distributed Switches	Chapter 2
Objective 2.3 – Configure vSS and vDS Policies	Chapter 2
Section 3 – Plan and Configure vSphere Storage	
Objective 3.1 – Configure Shared Storage for vSphere	Chapter 3
Objective 3.2 – Configure the Storage Virtual Appliance for vSphere	Chapter 3
Objective 3.3 – Create and Configure VMFS and NFS Datastores	Chapter 3
Section 4 – Deploy and Administer Virtual Machines and vApps	
Objective 4.1 – Create and Deploy Virtual Machines	Chapter 4
Objective 4.2 – Create and Deploy vApps	Chapter 4
Objective 4.3 – Manage Virtual Machine Clones and Templates	Chapter 4
Objective 4.4 – Administer Virtual Machines and vApps	Chapter 4
Section 5 – Establish and Maintain Service Levels	
Objective 5.1 – Create and Configure VMware Clusters	Chapter 5
Objective 5.2 – Plan and Implement VMware Fault Tolerance	Chapter 5
Objective 5.3 – Create and Administer Resource Pools	Chapter 5
Objective 5.4 – Migrate Virtual Machines	Chapter 5

Exam Section/Objective	Chapter Where Covered
Objective 5.5 – Backup and Restore Virtual Machines	Chapter 5
Objective 5.6 – Patch and Update ESXi and Virtual Machines	Chapter 5
Section 6 – Perform Basic Troubleshooting	
Objective 6.1 – Perform Basic Troubleshooting for ESXi Hosts	Chapter 6
Objective 6.2 – Perform Basic vSphere Network Troubleshooting	Chapter 6
Objective 6.3 – Perform Basic vSphere Storage Troubleshooting	Chapter 6
Objective 6.4 – Perform Basic Troubleshooting for HA/DRS Clusters and vMotion/Storage vMotion	Chapter 6
Section 7 – Monitor a vSphere Implementation and Manage vCenter Server Alarms	
Objective 7.1 – Monitor ESXi, vCenter Server and Virtual Machines	Chapter 7
Objective 7.2 – Create and Administer vCenter Server Alarms	Chapter 7

Book Content Updates

Because VMware occasionally updates exam topics without notice, VMware Press might post additional preparatory content on the web page associated with this book, at http://www.pearsonitcertification.com/title/9780789750181. It is a good idea to check the website a couple weeks before taking your exam to review any updated content that might be posted online. We also recommend that you periodically check back to this page on the Pearson IT Certification website to view any errata or supporting book files that may be available.

Pearson IT Certification Practice Test Engine and Questions on the DVD

The DVD in the back of this book includes the Pearson IT Certification Practice Test engine—software that displays and grades a set of exam-realistic multiple-choice questions. Using the Pearson IT Certification Practice Test engine, you can either study by going through the questions in Study Mode or take a simulated exam that mimics real exam conditions.

The installation process requires two major steps: installing the software and then activating the exam. The DVD in the back of this book has a recent copy of the Pearson IT Certification Practice Test engine. The practice exam—the database of exam questions—is not on the DVD.

NOTE The cardboard DVD case in the back of this book includes the DVD and a piece of paper. The paper lists the activation code for the practice exam associated with this book. *Do not lose the activation code.* On the opposite side of the paper from the activation code is a unique, one-time-use coupon code for the purchase of the Premium Edition eBook and Practice Test.

Install the Software from the DVD

The Pearson IT Certification Practice Test is a Windows-only desktop application. You can run it on a Mac using a Windows virtual machine, but it was built specifically for the PC platform. The minimum system requirements are as follows:

- Windows XP (SP3), Windows Vista (SP2), or Windows 7
- Microsoft .NET Framework 4.0 Client
- Microsoft SQL Server Compact 4.0
- Pentium-class 1GHz processor (or equivalent)
- 512 MB RAM
- 650 MB disc space plus 50 MB for each downloaded practice exam

The software installation process is pretty routine as compared with other software installation processes. You will need access to the Internet. If you have already installed the Pearson IT Certification Practice Test software from another Pearson product, there is no need for you to reinstall the software. Just launch the software on your desktop and proceed to activate the practice exam from this book by using the activation code included in the DVD sleeve.

The following steps outline the installation process:

1. Insert the DVD into your PC.
2. The software that automatically runs is the Pearson software to access and use all DVD-based features, including the exam engine and the DVD-only appendixes. In the main menu, click the Install the Exam Engine option.
3. Respond to window prompts, as with any typical software installation process.

The installation process gives you the option to activate your exam with the activation code supplied on the paper in the DVD sleeve. This process requires that you establish a Pearson website login. You need this login to activate the exam, so please register when prompted. If you already have a Pearson website login, there is no need to register again. Just use your existing login.

Activate and Download the Practice Exam

After installing the exam engine, you should then activate the exam associated with this book (if you did not do so during the installation process) as follows:

1. Start the Pearson IT Certification Practice Test software from the Windows Start menu or from your desktop shortcut icon.

2. To activate and download the exam associated with this book, in the My Products or Tools tab, click the Activate button.

3. At the next screen, enter the activation key from the paper inside the cardboard DVD sleeve in the back of the book. Then click the Activate button.

4. The activation process downloads the practice exam. Click Next and then click Finish.

When the activation process completes, the My Products tab should list your new exam. If you do not see the exam, make sure you have opened the My Products tab on the menu. At this point, the software and practice exam are ready to use. Simply select the exam and click the Open Exam button.

To update a particular exam you have already activated and downloaded, open the Tools tab and click the Update Products button. Updating your exams will ensure you have the latest changes and updates to the exam data.

If you want to check for updates to the Pearson Cert Practice Test exam engine software, open the Tools tab and click the Update Application button. This will ensure you are running the latest version of the software engine.

Activating Other Exams

The exam software installation process, like the registration process, has to happen only once. Then, for each new exam, only a few steps are required. For instance, if you buy another new Pearson IT Certification Guide or VMware Press Official Certification Guide, extract the activation code from the DVD sleeve in the back of that book; you do not even need the DVD at that point. From there, all you have to do is start the exam engine (if it is not already up and running) and perform steps 2 through 4 from the previous list.

Premium Edition

In addition to the free practice exam provided on the DVD, you can purchase two additional exams with expanded functionality directly from Pearson IT Certification. The Premium Edition eBook and Practice Test for this title contains an additional full practice exam and an eBook (in both PDF and ePub format). In addition, the Premium Edition title also has remediation for each question to the specific part of the eBook that relates to that question.

If you have purchased the print version of this title, you can purchase the Premium Edition at a deep discount. A coupon code in the DVD sleeve contains a one-time-use code and instructions for where you can purchase the Premium Edition.

To view the Premium Edition product page, go to
http://www.pearsonitcertification.com/title/9780133125351.

This chapter covers the following subjects:

- **What Is a Technical Design?** This section explains what a technical design is and why it is important to the end solution.

- **The Technical Design Process:** This section demonstrates what happens at each stage of the technical design process.

- **Project Deliverables:** This section covers what should be produced as part of a technical design, such as the documents, sample contents, and so on.

This chapter covers the following portion of the VCAP5-DCD 5 blueprint:

Section 1, "Create a vSphere conceptual design."

CHAPTER 1

Introduction to Technical Design

Technical design requires completely different skills from the troubleshooting and maintenance tasks commonly carried out by experienced IT professionals. The role of a technical designer or architect involves communication skills, technical knowledge, and a certain amount of artistic flare. This chapter will take you through the terminology and process of technical design. The concepts discussed here can be applied to any project, not just a VMware-related solution. By understanding and working with a design process, an engineer can integrate with other business and technical professionals and provide valued input to a business project.

"Do I Know This Already?" Quiz

The "Do I Know This Already?" quiz allows you to assess whether you should read this entire chapter or simply jump to the "Exam Preparation Tasks" section for review. If you are in doubt, read the entire chapter. Table 1-1 outlines the major headings in this chapter and the corresponding "Do I Know This Already?" quiz questions. You can find the answers in Appendix A, "Answers to the 'Do I Know Already?' Quizzes and 'Q&A' Chapter Review Questions."

Table 1-1 "Do I Know This Already?" Foundation Topics Section-to-Question Mapping

Foundations Topics Section	Questions Covered in This Section
What Is a Technical Design?	1, 7, 9, 12
The Technical Design Process	2–4, 6, 10
Project Deliverables	5, 8, 11, 13

1. Which of the following is a design methodology?

    a. A set of best practices for the technology

    b. An iterative process used to produce a technical solution

    c. A project proposal that shows the advantages of new technology or the latest upgrade

2. Which of the following is a project risk?

    a. The technology is over three years old.

    b. The technology is cutting edge.

    c. Both a and b.

3. Who sets the vision?

    a. The board and business professionals

    b. IT staff

    c. A proposed vendor

4. Who generally sets the scope?

    a. Business staff

    b. IT staff and business staff working together

    c. The proposed vendor

5. Which of the following is true of a project requirement?

    a. It must be satisfied.

    b. It is for advice and observation only.

    c. Both a and b

6. You are working on a project team tasked to migrate a platform between two datacenters. Which of the following describes a design methodology?

    a. A set of best practices for the technology

    b. An iterative process used to produce a technical solution

    c. A project proposal that shows the advantages of new technology or latest upgrade

7. Which of the following describes a best practice?

    a. Dictated by the vendor as the way to do something

    b. Continuously evolving

    c. Static

8. If changed, which of the following may affect the logical design?

   a. The server vendor

   b. The type of replication from synchronous to asynchronous

   c. The IP addresses of the servers

9. A project vision may be a long-term goal, and it may be achieved after several iterations of a project life cycle.

   a. True

   b. False

10. Which of the following is a constraint on design?

    a. The VDI platform is dependent on a stable network, which is not managed by the internal network team.

    b. The VDI project has a small budget.

    c. During a migration project, the destination datacenter has not been completely finished. It is currently three months behind schedule.

11. The number of disks used in a storage array is detailed in the physical design.

    a. True

    b. False

12. You are the technical lead in a vSphere 4 to vSphere 5 project. The platform is currently using a supported NFS storage device. There are no plans to upgrade or change this device within two years. Which of the following is correct?

    a. This is a risk to the project.

    b. This is a design constraint.

    c. This is a design assumption.

13. Best practices can be used as guidance in a design, assuming that the requirements are satisfied.

    a. True

    b. False

Foundation Topics

What Is a Technical Design?

A technical design is a way of communicating an end product or solution. By creating a technical design, a group of people can work together to create a final solution.

A design methodology is a multiphase process used to direct a technical design process. A design process is:

- Iterative
- Involves other people
- Helpful and necessary to the success of a project

Where Do We Start? What Are We Doing?

These questions are asked not only in the classroom but also during real projects. Skilled engineers are accustomed to some form of guidance, such as a vendor best practice or a design document from an experienced consultant or architect. How are technical designs constructed? How does an engineer bridge the gap between engineer and architect/designer?

What Makes a Good Designer?

I have asked this question in a number of training courses. The following are some examples of responses:

- Expertise—in-depth technical knowledge
- Experience—someone who has implemented the technology previously
- Good communication—a technical expert who can talk to nontechnical people

From my own commercial experience, I know that a good designer is someone who can:

- Accept advice from other members of the team and other stakeholders
- Be flexible to change and understand that the end result is the required aim
- Acquire new skills rapidly

Most importantly, however, a good designer questions everything!

For example, say that a technical designer working on an application migration project interviews a senior user who spends 40 hours per week operating a data processing application. The user has data delivered to him weekly as a zip file. He unzips the file, counts the number of uncompressed files, and takes a copy for an archive and uploads it into the system. He stores the zip file in one folder (original) and keeps a copy of the unzipped files in another (imported data).

The designer establishes that this method is viewed as the accepted process—the company best practice, which has been developed over time by an experienced member of staff.

A technical designer would probe this process from various angles, asking questions such as: When is the data required? Can the zip file be stored and unzipped when required? Is it possible to work backward from the result of the data processing?" The zip file is a smaller copy of the processed data after all, and even a designer with no experience with the software at the user level could save the company time and money by taking a step back and questioning the process—even if it is an accepted one.

A Familiar Scenario...?

Suppose that a company's CTO calls his team into a meeting. The CTO looks enthusiastic and says, "I've just had a meeting with the board. Our competitors are gaining on us. We need to deploy our services more rapidly, without lowering the quality our customers expect. The web applications are needed now rather than next quarter."

The CTO continues, "I need the platform guys to continue to support the production system but work smarter, so you can spend more time with the development team and investigating new technology. Developers, I am depending on you to produce our new software on time. Automate it all. You are the top team! If you make this work, there will be no more late nights in the office! And one more thing: Nobody mention a budget!"

The CTO leaves the room, the dust settles, and the project team looks at each other. Now what?

The Technical Design Process

Key Topic

Try typing "design methodology" into a web search engine. You will be presented with numerous versions and definitions. Some of these definitions are standard, but some are company specific. VMware, for example, has developed its own methodology, called VIM, for Virtual Infrastructure Methodology.

Each methodology has various pros and cons, but all have similar phases:

- Information gathering—This is where a problem, vision, or goal is described; requirements are detailed; users are interviewed; and factors affecting the project, such as risks, constraints, compliancy, and cost are highlighted. Analysis of the current state of play is carried out.

- Solution development—This phase uses the information gathered from the previous phase to produce a detailed solution.

- Implementation and delivery—This stage utilizes the detailed plans from the solution development phase, and the solution is produced.

- Review and manage—During this frequently forgotten part of the technical design process, the project and solution are discussed to ensure quality and continuous improvement. Issues such as ongoing maintenance and operational management can be addressed here.

The basic components of a good design are:

- Vision

- Scope

- Requirements

- Constraints

- Assumptions

- Risks

Vision

The vision component represents the actual idea—the light bulb over the cartoon character—and is the whole reason for a project. The vision must, therefore, be kept at the forefront throughout the project.

The vision may be ambitious, such as "Automate everything."

The project team might never actually achieve the original vision; costs, risks, and constraints could prevent it. The vision is the end goal; however, without a vision, a project may evolve into something else entirely.

The vision is normally set or controlled at the upper management level, and it is, consequently, a business-driven attribute rather than one driven by technology.

Scope

The scope is a quantitative statement of what is included in a project, or, more pertinently, what is not included in a project.

While virtualization consolidation projects may have several phases, instead of trying to virtualize every machine in the company in one go, the scope would specify quick wins or good, critical, or high-priority candidates, allowing for progress on the project while establishing implementation methods.

The project requester normally creates the project scope, but he or she further develops it by working with other members of the project team, such as IT management.

Requirements

A requirement is an attribute that must be achieved; for example, the solution must comply with the company's security policy, the current security policy specifies that any web-facing application servers must be separate from internal application servers.

Requirements affect design choice substantially.

Constraints

A constraint is an attribute that may limit a design choice, and it could be technical or business driven. For example, in a datacenter migration project, the storage vendor has already been decided due to existing company vendor relationships. This choice means that data de-duplication technology cannot be used, as it is not available from the preferred vendor. A greater amount of network bandwidth would be required to synchronize data between the two sites.

Consider the applications running on the new virtual platform; a requirement states that these applications must remain supported by the application vendor. If the vendor does not support applications running in VMware platforms, the application may have to remain running on physical machines.

Assumptions

An assumption is something that has been decided to be true for the project design but that has not been tested nor verified.

Say that a company requires a new remote working solution. It creates a project and assembles a team. The current solution, a VPN, is provided by an outsourcing company. This service was already in place before a firm-wide agreement of telecommuting was in place. The contracts in place prevent renegotiation of service until next year. There is, however, no reason to expect an issue as the availability and performance of the VPN have been acceptable. Therefore, a suitable assumption could be "Sufficient network bandwidth to support 500 concurrent VDI users is available via the existing VPN solution." It could be difficult to accurately predict the amount of network bandwidth required and the work patterns of the proposed service once in use.

Risks

A risk is an attribute that could prevent the completion of a project or change the project design considerably.

Risks can be pretty easy to spot. For example, say that in a datacenter migration project, one datacenter is being demolished, and another one is being constructed. The company has to move in any case, and it is starting the application migration project before the destination datacenter is available. If the availability of the second site is delayed, the project will be affected substantially. This is a risk.

A less obvious risk would be using cutting-edge technology. Has this been done by someone else, on this scale? If not, it may not be the best solution.

Project Deliverables

Depending on the size and type of project or the organization where the project is being carried out, the items that are delivered from the project process will vary. They could include the following:

- A high-level design document (HLD)
- A quick one-pager
- A proof-of-concept solution
- An implementation or configuration document
- A test or verification document
- Support documentation

At a minimum, it is useful to always have a short HLD that explains the approach. In addition, a quick one-pager or a data flow diagram is an invaluable reference during project meetings and defenses. A good example of such a diagram is an exit plan affixed near the elevator in case of fire or other emergency.

Talking through a design with a CTO is a completely different task than talking through a system with another designer or a technical resource. The technical details of the design have to be pitched correctly; you must present useful information with sufficient detail to ensure comfort in the project or confidence in the design.

If a suitable level of communication is not achieved and maintained, there is a danger of confusion, scope creep, and an unsuccessful project.

Building a Realistic and Executable Plan of Approach

Following the information gathering phase, you can devise a realistic time frame and approach for the project. A key question to address is whether the project will be delivered in one big bang or in smaller, more manageable phases.

For example, in a recent vCloud project, I was required to deploy a secure and scalable hybrid cloud platform to release various e-discovery applications. It was possible, of course, to plan to make all applications available to users simultaneously, releasing nothing until all the project requirements were met. This approach requires a huge investment in terms of technical hours, and if the finished application does not meet user expectations, you have to start over.

A less risky approach is to separate the requirements into phases, with each phase working toward the vision. In the vCloud project I worked on, we used the following phases:

1. **Vendor selection**—In selecting the VMware datacenter hosting provider, we considered the requirements detailed in the information gathering phase.

2. **Proof of concept application**—We produced a proof of concept based on the solution design. The application the users were most familiar with was selected as the first candidate, and it was used to establish the process for verification and validation of the design.

3. **Production deployment of application**—Based on the lessons learned from the proof of concept, we released a single production application.

4. **Integration and management**—We implemented the support and operational management requirements.

Once phase 3 was complete, additional applications were deployed, using the processes developed from the first live deployment. Gradually we released all applications and created a full production platform with associated management and integration tools.

This phased release approach gave comfort to the business sponsor, who was able to witness regular application releases on a tight schedule. This staggered approach provided the opportunity for continuous platform improvements from one release to the next.

General Guidelines for a Good Technical Design

Although every project is different and depends on several factors, a good technical design should:

- Be simple and easy to reproduce
- Be scalable
- Be cost efficient
- Be fault tolerant
- Have a total cost of ownership that the business can achieve
- Be supportable

One useful addition to every technical design is a section that justifies the design choices and references the original requirements, constraints, risks, and so on. This extra information demonstrates to the business project sponsor that all the requirements have been seriously considered, and it also assists the designer in validating his or her thought process at the next project iteration.

Learning from Experience

How do you know if a project has been successful?

Early in my career as a Windows engineer, I worked on many Microsoft Exchange projects. Microsoft Exchange can be deployed in various ways, and it does have some great functionality. For instance, I remember well the excitement surrounding the release of Outlook Anywhere, and the massive impact it had. Users were suddenly able to double-click on an icon and check email without a VPN! The underlying system, however, was not completely fault tolerant, and the single points of failure were unlikely to satisfy uptime requirements if they failed.

This is an example of a project evolving from "Building a highly available messaging solution for the company based on a standard supportable platform" to "Enabling users to access email from any location without the use of a VPN."

As you work on a project, ensure that at every stage of the project, the vision and requirements remain in clear view. It is easy to lose sight of the vision or goal and fall prey to scope creep. Both the vision and requirements should be clearly defined and not open to interpretation.

Measuring Project Success

"That will do." This everyday saying makes many people shudder; however, it can be very true with technical design.

A company needs a sensible design to be delivered on time and within budget, and it needs the design to meet requirements while observing risks and assumptions and operating around constraints.

"True perfection has to be imperfect; I know that sounds foolish, but it's true."

—Noel Gallagher

Your project may be far from perfect, but if it meets its vision while respecting all requirements, then it can be regarded as a success. Any imperfections can be fixed either as a business-as-usual exercise or during a period of stabilization.

Exam Preparation Tasks

Review All Key Topics

Review the most important topics in the chapter, noted with the key topics icon in the outer margin of the page. Table 1-2 lists these key topics and the page number on which each is found.

Table 1-2 Key Topics

Key Topic Element	Description	Page
Paragraph	The Technical Design Process	7
Paragraph	Building a Realistic and Executable Plan of Approach	11
List	General Guidelines for a Good Technical Design	12

Design Scenarios

Create your own standard templates for a high-level design process:

- Write down the components of a design process as headings in a document.

- Think of a project you have worked on as an engineer. Fill in each component area with bullet points to consider. This is the start of your HLD.

- Start to flesh out the HLD. Add more detail, such as what your company's security policy specifies with regard to encryption, uptime, and so on.

- Use the HLD to create a one-page summary of the project. Construct a diagram of the solution. (Logical and physical designs are discussed in Chapter 4, "Developing a Design on Paper and Delivering It Physically")

- The skills needed for these tasks are assumed in the VCAP5-DCD exam.

Definitions of Key Terms

Define the following key terms from this chapter and check your answers in the glossary.

Vision, Requirement, Constraint, Risk, Assumption

Read the Technical Material with a Designer's Hat On

- No specifically defined or examined design process exists for the VCAP5-DCD; you must adapt a suitable one with which to work throughout your exam preparation.

- Study the recommended reading on the VCAP5-DCD blueprint, ensuring that you work to the latest exam version; slight changes in documentation or content often appear without warning.

- Although the VCAP5-DCD exam is a highly technical one, try to look past the technical facts and consider the impact of the settings or functionalities. For example, do not simply memorize the requirements for vMotion but consider the effect of guest virtual machines not meeting those vMotion requirements. Will the cluster become imbalanced? What is the importance of initial guest placement? What affect will DRS have?

- Know the VMware design terminology. Technical knowledge is great, but this exam also requires you to understand business requirements. If you don't have experience with design work, remember to ask questions such as, "Is this the best way? Is it still simple? Is it required? Does its meet the requirements?"

Review Questions

The answers to these review questions are in Appendix A.

1. You are working on a hybrid cloud project, where production applications (yet to be fully developed) are to be deployed. Which of the following is a project requirement?

    a. The production data must be in the UK at all times.

    b. The hosting partner provides sufficient resources, without overcommitting, to support application load.

    c. The hosting provider meets uptime expectations.

    d. The development team provides the software on time.

2. In the project life cycle, who defines the vision?

    a. The IT architect

    b. The software vendor

    c. The business

3. Which of the following describes an item that is taken to be true at the design phase but has not been tested prior to execution?

    a. Requirement

    b. Constraint

    c. Assumption

    d. Risk

4. You are a virtualization consultant working on a disaster recovery project. You have proposed a solution that uses SAN technology to replicate production virtual machine files. This meets a cold standby requirement. During a design workshop meeting several points are raised. Which of the following could be a design constraint?

    a. The hardware currently being used in the datacenter is no longer supported.

    b. The company is undecided about the choice of centralized storage to be used in the enterprise.

    c. The company is at the end of year one of a three-year contract for the point-to-point link between site A and site B. This link is currently 10MB.

5. You are a technical consultant designing a solution for a web retail company. The project vision is to deploy a hybrid cloud, where the internal team develops the website on internal infrastructure and migrates production-ready applications to a hosting provider. The project is expected to ease deployment and require less infrastructure capital expenditure without lowering application quality. Which of the following is a risk associated with the project?

  a. The solution must adhere to ISO27001.

  b. Change control of the hosting vCloud platform is not under full control of the internal business.

  c. The hosting provider outsources the platform support to the platform vendor.

  d. The applications to be deployed are not fully developed, although a beta exists.

6. A project vision in some cases may not be achieved due to constraints, risks, and other project factors. However, a vision is required to guide the project throughout the life cycle.

  a. True

  b. False

7. When should a software vendor's best practice be adhered to? (Choose all that apply.)

  a. Whenever possible, respecting other project requirements

  b. At all times because the vendor wrote and designed the software

  c. When there are no other requirements, as a guide to configuration

8. The following diagrams may be included in project documentation. Which of them shows a system's components and how they could affect each other?

  a. Logical

  b. Entity relationship diagram

  c. Physical diagram

This chapter covers the following subjects:

- **Gathering Information and Spotting the Gaps:** This section explains how to start a project from a technical design perspective.

- **Presenting the Data Gathered:** This section covers what should be produced as part of the information gathering and logical design phase.

- **Real-Life Tips:** This section explains the processes to follow when gathering information and the types of information to collect.

This chapter covers the following objectives of the VCAP5-DCD blueprint:

Objective 1.2, "Gather and analyze application requirements"

Objective 2.1, "Map business requirements to the logical design"

Objective 2.2, "Map service dependencies"

Objective 2.5, "Build performance requirements into the logical design"

CHAPTER 2

Creating a Design

Following a design process or methodology helps a project team work efficiently together, but where does a virtualization architect actually start?

Gathering information on the environment, understanding the vision, and analyzing key information from the current platform and from fellow project and departmental stakeholders helps you establish the gap between the vision and the start of the project. From this analysis, you can create the technical approach, milestones, and a logical design.

"Do I Know This Already?" Quiz

The "Do I Know This Already?" quiz allows you to assess whether you should read this entire chapter or simply jump to the "Exam Preparation Tasks" section for review. If you are in doubt, read the entire chapter. Table 2-1 outlines the major headings in this chapter and the corresponding "Do I Know This Already?" quiz questions. You can find the answers in Appendix A, "Answers to the 'Do I Know This Already?' Quizzes and Chapter Review Questions."

Table 2-1 "Do I Know This Already?" Foundation Topics Section-to-Question Mapping

Foundations Topics Section	Questions Covered in This Section
Gathering Information	1–4, 7
Presenting the Data	8, 9, 10
Approach & Design Process	5, 6

1. Which of the following types of discovery methods require agents?

   a. Active

   b. Passive

   c. Both a and b

2. Which of the following types of discovery methods is most likely to impact the platform it is discovering?

   a. Active

   b. Passive

   c. Both a and b

3. Which of the following tools can be used to survey a physical platform with the intention to migrate to a virtual platform?

   a. VMware ThinApp

   b. VMware vCenter

   c. VMware Capacity Planner

4. Which of the following tools can be used to collect relevant data on physical and virtual platforms and provide automated relationship entity diagrams?

   a. VMware vCenter Application Discovery Manager

   b. VMware vCenter Server

5. Which of the following does an entity relationship diagram show?

   a. The physical attributes of a platform and their dependencies

   b. The virtual attributes of a platform and their dependencies

   c. The logical components of a platform and their dependencies

6. In a multitier website, consisting of a web front end, a processing midtier, and a database back end, what will happen to the downstream components if the web tier fails?

   a. The downstream components will be unaffected by the web tier.

   b. The downstream components will be unavailable.

7. A current state analysis allows the project team to have a clear understanding of the platform at project initiation.

    a. True

    b. False

8. A current state analysis can create more requirements.

    a. True

    b. False

9. How is a gap state analysis used?

    a. To create a list of tasks required to reach the vision

    b. To ensure that all aspects of the platform have been identified

10. How are requirements obtained?

    a. The business manager or project sponsor obtains them.

    b. The team completes an information gathering exercise such as a gap state analysis.

    c. Both a and b

Foundation Topic

Gathering Information and Spotting the Gaps

With today's access to countless resources, simply typing a few keywords into a search engine will undoubtedly present you with examples of designs and case studies for virtualization solutions. It could be very easy (and tempting) to simply implement a design from a previous case study or engineer blog site. The result could, in fact, be the correct solution. But how do you prevent errors and ensure that the solution satisfies the requirements and reaches the desired vision? You can start by doing the following:

- Gather information from key systems and stakeholders

- Establish dependencies and identify conflicts

- Create a logical technical approach

- Create the logical design

Consider the following scenario: Say that you are the virtualization consultant at ModStyle Clothing Inc. You have been hired to design and lead, from a technical perspective, a consolidation project to reduce the number of datacenters at from five to two. The high-level information from the hiring manager and CTO states that the company is following a virtualize-first policy and is aggressively virtualizing all systems wherever possible. Currently the scope of the project is concerned with the customer-facing website rather than backend systems.

How do you proceed? Do you walk in on day 1 and aggressively convert all servers from physical to virtual, starting with the first server in the first rack nearest the door?

The brief from the hiring process is insufficient to start technical work, but it does give the overall vision and indication of the project attitude: Reduce datacenters and virtualize first! So, if you follow a more logical route, a good starting point is to consider a few technical approaches (there are many more that can be discussed here):

- **A physical-to-virtual conversion**—Start with the current platform and produce virtualized systems.

- **A rebuild and switchover**—Using knowledge of the current platform, rebuild the systems from scratch within a virtual environment.

- **A scale-out and decommission**—Expand the current system with duplicate or redundant server roles within the virtual environment. Once the virtual machine is configured, power down and remove the legacy/physical system.

All three options are viable and seem technically possible. The issue here is deciding which of these options is best for the specific project. By asking questions and gathering relevant data, you should be able to decide on a suitable technical approach and create a logical design for the project.

By taking stock of where you are starting, you will undoubtedly understand the environment better, and in some cases you might uncover items that could change the plan. Figure 2-1 shows an example of a current state analysis.

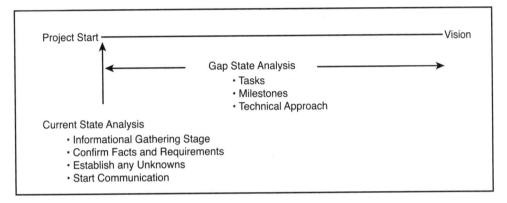

Figure 2-1   A Current State Analysis

A current state analysis gives an architect a way to examine the road ahead. Any oversights at this stage could have major implications for the project later on. By ensuring that the current state analysis is completed thoroughly, you can prevent many potential problems.

Data such as the following may be gathered for a current state analysis:

- Number of sites, servers, or devices

- A list of applications and their dependencies

- Current use and capacity

- Known issues (for example, a specific piece of software is not supported in a virtualized platform, an application requires certain hardware to run)

- Forthcoming projects and future growth plan (for example, Will extra capacity be needed soon? Is a critical point in the business year approaching?)

- Licensing, support, and maintenance information

- Business standards, policies, and compliance information

Selecting the Best Tool for the Job

From simple manual tools to elaborate automated monitoring applications, various tools are available for gathering the information for a current state analysis:

- Windows Perfmon

- VMware vCenter Performance Graphs

- Monitoring solutions such as Nagios and SolarWinds

- VMware Capacity Planner tool

- VMware vCenter Application Discovery Manager

There are two main types of discovery methods:

- **Active discovery**—This is a method where the monitoring platform runs processes that may have a detrimental effect on the target discovery component. The monitoring processes are set to run at regular intervals (such as every 2 minutes). For example, when monitoring a multitier website in this manner to discover the average page response time, the process could increase load on the server and, therefore, lengthen the page response time. In such a case, the statistics obtained through this method would be invalid. Also, this method may require the use of monitoring agents installed on the target servers. These agents also use additional resources, such as CPU and memory, and, if not considered, could invalidate the statistics.

  The one main advantage of active discovery methods is simplicity. Software of this type can normally be installed quickly and can be left running to gather information and produce standard reports with minimal hands-on effort.

- **Passive discovery**—In passive discovery, data is obtained by non-intrusive means, such as port mirroring. Agents do not need to be installed on target servers. This method may be preferable for complex production platforms that are under high change control and security review. Interpreting the data with this method requires greater experience and skill than the active discovery method.

Which is the best method? It depends on the situation.

The scale of the project and the critical path to deliver the vision will help guide you in selecting a tool. If a system is entirely physical, and capacity planning is more manual, tools such as Perfmon would provide useful statistics. Data from such tools, however, might be hard to aggregate and interpret.

Experience with a tool is another key factor. For advanced information gathering applications, the tool may be capable of automatically mapping dependencies and providing perfect selection of metrics required to make decisions. In some cases, this tool could provide recommendations on things like the number of hosts required.

Ideally, the information gathering stage should last at least one period of standard activity. For example, a month in a business would show the normal month-end batch processing, pay cycle for staff, and so on. The risks would be events such as end-of-year tasks. This is where your interpretation of the data and business comes in. Ensure that you know how your users interact with the services you provide and ensure that you are familiar with key business dates and initiatives. How do you get this information if you are from the technical department or a third-party contractor? A key aspect of this stage in the project is stakeholder review. Virtualization touches all parts of the datacenter and is extremely flexible. It's so flexible, in fact, that it is fairly easy to have multiple projects rolled up into one virtualization project. The key is to understand and be aware of extra requirements.

In our example, the CTO has decided that the best strategy is "virtualize first." The current production platform is completely physical: one service, one server. For every logical component there is another redundant component. The vision is a fully virtual deployment, with applications running on a stable and protected infrastructure.

The reality, though, is that due to a recent managerial change and the new strategy, the company has not invested in the current infrastructure for a considerable time. There is also increasing pressure from the business to be able to react to current competition, and the business's peak season is only three months away. Suddenly this project is not happening in a silo; every other project is now dependent on it.

The website needs to be ready for peak season. To be successful, new parts or functions of the website need to be operational by the same deadline. However, the development team has yet to finish writing those new parts or functions and is waiting for a development and test platform.

The current development and test platform consists of a couple of physical boxes that are out of support, running legacy software, and in dire need of a refresh, which has been delayed due to the upcoming virtual platform being implemented. To ensure that there are no more unexpected surprises at this stage, it is important to include all relevant stakeholders in your design interviews.

Presenting the Data Gathered

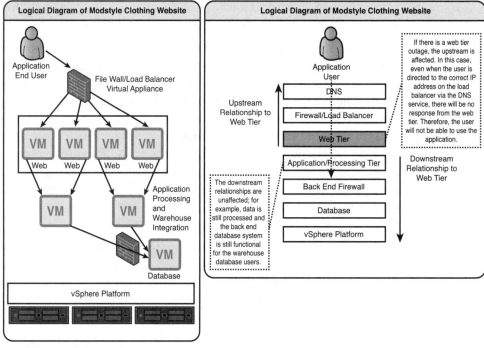

Figure 2-2 Logical and Component Relationship Diagrams

The following are some examples of notes the designer made based on interviews:

- **CTO**—Virtualize-first strategy. Ideally, looking for 100% virtual within 1 year. IT cost savings in 3 years, with faster deployment times. Looking to lower operating costs from project execution. Has promised the business the ability to provide a stable and scalable platform for the business.

- **Development manager**—Agrees with the virtualize-first strategy. However, by having hands-on knowledge of the current system, is aware of key issues that will need to be addressed by the developers. The physical production system will not support the additional functionality required due to memory constraints and the requirement of 64-bit operating systems (because of third-party application components). All development and test systems are currently 32-bit, except for two workstations that are used for source control, build, and deployment functions for new projects.

- **Operations manager**—The team is under incredible pressure. Following a management change, the support team has decreased from 21 people of various abilities to 9 senior engineers. The amount of work in the current platform is very resource intensive. The operations manager requires a stable, self-managing platform to give the analysts sufficient time to work with developers and deploy the new functionality.

- **Application manager**—Owns and is responsible for the application being used by the business end users. The functionality roadmap is available and is very important. Key competitors have already released more advanced platforms; however, they have been hit by performance issues. The functionality of a new platform needs to be tested as early as possible.

Technical Approach, Building Task Lists, and Implementation Order

After you combine the current state analysis, the project requirements, and the stakeholder interviews, you can create a task list and form an implementation plan.

TIP   It is critical to be able to categorize the requirements, risks, and constraints from interview summaries. You also need to be able to spot areas of conflict and potential problems.

In our example, the vision is the key deliverable. It is a scalable platform to ensure that the business can compete in the marketplace. New projects could be required in relatively short time frames; however, quality is of utmost importance.

Although the project brief states that the virtualize-first aspect is key, and server consolidation is a prime activity, the development manager is aware of technical reasons this may not work. In addition, a test may not be possible due to a lack of appropriate machines.

The operations manager and application manager appear to be extremely busy with business-as-usual tasks, and they are under pressure to deliver platforms for the new functionality.

Key Points from the Summary of Stakeholder Interviews

Virtualize first and high consolidation are project requirements; however, conflicting information is present and needs attention.

There is no suitable test bed for virtualized copies of the production systems. A physical-to-virtual conversion on some of the systems will not work in the long term due to the 32-bit systems needing to be rebuilt with 64-bit operating systems. This change will need to be scheduled at an appropriate time, or duplication of work will occur.

The teams have a possible capacity issue on the current platform and are under pressure with staff resources to provide new functionality. Testing is very important.

Milestone Plan and Technical Approach

Following the information gathering stage, the required number of hosts, CPU memory, and sufficient bandwidth and storage I/O are selected. Based on the stakeholder interviews, the following approach is determined: The vision will be achieved in a phased approach. Each phase will provide part of the solution and serve as a foundation for the next. The development and test systems will be created on a vSphere platform to ensure that all other teams can work and deliver their requirements. Based on lessons learned, the production platform will then be delivered, enabling a fully functional and scalable virtual environment.

Milestone Phases

The team needs to create a vSphere platform for the development and test systems first. This will provide the developers and operations staff time to test and learn to support the new functionality.

Based on processes and builds from phase 1, the team will create a scalable production platform. This will allow the team to build and test production applications with new functionality. Templates and processes derived from phases 1 and 2 will allow rapid creation of platform components and scaling going forward.

Following a successful test, the team will decommission the original 32-bit platform.

Justification for Design Choices

You should always be sure to include your justifications and selection criteria in your logical design documents. These justifications are useful to have when you explain your approach during design and milestone meetings, and they ensure that you are aware of the impact of the technical approach and the components of the platform or solution you are building.

Although the current production platform can be technically consolidated into a virtual platform, the project is providing a platform for long-term applications. These applications require different operating systems than current production servers and therefore require testing.

A physical-to-virtual consolidation exercise would result in a short-term gain of consolidation benefits (for example, costs, space). However, it can cause delays in the other departments waiting for 64-bit operating systems. This consolidation would also require work to be duplicated when the new systems are put in place.

If the team deploys a new test and develops a 64-bit platform, the new functionality can be coded, supported, and, based on this learning phase, allow the production platform to be deployed using proven processes.

Real-Life Tips

Consider deploying projects in stages to give stakeholders confidence in moving forward. Justifying project budgets is difficult. Managers will be happier to see progress, however small, than an all-or-nothing approach. A staged approach allows more time to fix issues or requirement misunderstandings, as the solution is shown to the stakeholders earlier.

Establish enthusiasm for your project. Interested users who like gadgets or IT make great testers. Create a test plan to ensure that aspects within scope are covered.

Communication is key to the business. Create a weekly update or involve the users with information on how the system will help them. An internal project website with the latest documents, drawings, and even videos will help create good dialogue.

Exam Preparation Tasks

Review All Key Topics

Review the most important topics in the chapter, noted with the key topics icon in the outer margin of the page. Table 2-2 lists these key topics and the page number on which each is found.

Table 2-2 Key Topics

Key Topic Element	Description	Page
List	Tools for gathering information in a current state analysis	24
Paragraph	Active and passive discovery methods	24
Figure 2-2	Presenting the data gathered	26
Paragraph	Justification for design choices	28

Design Scenario

Practice creating logical diagrams and establishing relationships. Follow these steps:

1. Consider a key application from your current workplace or on a system you have supported in the past. Consider the user and business expectations for normal uptime and the potential impact if the system were out of action.

2. Summarize the user expectations as a service-level agreement for the IT department. Consider RTO and RPO.

3. Draw a logical design based on the working implementation.

4. Separate the application into key components.

5. Establish the upstream and downstream relationships to the components. Draw a diagram and table to show the relationships.

6. Consider how to improve the solution and create a desired implementation.

7. List the tasks to achieve the final solution.

8. Consider the order in which to complete the tasks and use a phased approach.

9. List the phases and tasks as milestones in the plan.

10. Prepare a presentation or a short walkthrough document to describe the subject.

Definitions of Key Terms

Define the following key terms from this chapter and check your answers in the glossary.

Upstream relationship, Downstream relationship, Functional requirement, Current state analysis, Gap state analysis

Review Questions

The answers to these review questions are in Appendix A.

1. In a multitier website consisting of a web front end, a processing midtier, and a database backend, what will happen to the upstream components if the database tier fails?

    a. The upstream components are unaffected by the database tier.

    b. The upstream components will be unavailable.

2. A design choice must be:

   a. Justified

   b. As cost-effective as possible

   c. Specified in a requirement

3. You are a VMware architect attending a project kickoff meeting. The project vision is to "consolidate all existing physical workloads to a vSphere 5 platform." The high-level requirements are defined during the design kickoff meeting. Which of the following is true?

   a. You should make design choices based on current best practices and case studies from previous vendor implementations.

   b. You should review the current server estate to ensure the viability of the project in relation to the requirements and establish the tasks required to achieve the vision.

   c. You should construct a logical and physical design, based on requirements and guide best practices from previous implementations in the community.

4. Which of the following can a gap state analysis help achieve?

   a. The vision

   b. The logical design

   c. A list of best practices

5. Which of the following type of discovery methods is least likely to impact the platform it is discovering?

   a. Active

   b. Passive

6. A component relationship diagram can be used to establish the order of component change or impact analysis.

   a. True

   b. False

7. Which of the following tools would enable a Windows administrator to complete a state analysis of a virtual Windows 2008 Server guest machine without requiring access to the vSphere platform?

   a. VMware Perfmon DLL

   b. resxtop

   c. PowerCLI monitor script

This chapter covers the following subjects:

- **What Makes a Good Choice for Virtualization, and What Is a Good Design?** This section discusses what a designer should consider when developing a design for a virtual workload, as well as general good design practice.

- **"It's Okay, We Have HA!"** This section discusses the importance and impact of RTO and RPO requirements.

- **Platform and Operations: The Roles:** This section discusses the importance of designing a solution that suits the business and that the IT function can support and manage.

This chapter covers the following objectives from the VCAP5-DCD blueprint:

- Objective 2.3, "Build availability requirements into the logical design"

- Objective 2.4, "Build manageability requirements into the logical design objective"

- Objective 2.5, "Build performance requirements into the logical design"

- Objective 2.6, "Build recoverability requirements into the logical design"

- Objective 2.7, "Build security requirements into the logical design"

CHAPTER 3

Thoughts on Good Choices for Virtualization and Design

The numerous advantages that virtualization brings to a datacenter have impacted expectations and attitudes in many businesses. IT strategies such as "virtualize first" and "virtualize everything" are commonplace. However, many CTOs and chief architects can swiftly change their minds to "physical everything" if applications have not performed as expected. As a technical architect, you may often find yourself stuck between the business and the operations guys and engineers.

A technical architect must understand the high-level business requirements and translate them into technical designs—while ensuring data security, ease of use, and other key aspects.

"Do I Know This Already?" Quiz

The "Do I Know This Already?" quiz allows you to assess whether you should read this entire chapter or simply jump to the "Exam Preparation Tasks" section for review. If you are in doubt, read the entire chapter. Table 3-1 outlines the major headings in this chapter and the corresponding "Do I Know This Already?" quiz questions. You can find the answers in Appendix A, "Answers to the 'Do I Know This Already?' and Chapter Review Questions."

Table 3-1 "Do I Know This Already?" Foundation Topics Section-to-Question Mapping

Foundations Topics Section	Questions Covered in This Section
What Makes a Good Choice for Virtualization, and What Is a Good Design?	7
"It's Okay, We Have HA!"	1–3, 6, 8, 9
Platform and Operation: The Roles	4, 5, 10

1. VMware HA can provide seamless application business continuity on the platform layer.

   a. True

   b. False

2. The infrastructure qualities are a list of attributes that can be used to ensure that major aspects are considered and help with good design processes. Which of the following are the infrastructure qualities?

   a. RTO, RPO, and mean time between failures

   b. Availability, manageability, performance, recoverability, and security

   c. Capacity, change control, security, DR, and supportability

3. What is mean time between failures?

   a. The mean of the total outages of a service in a defined period (for example, 1 year)

   b. The average time between service failures

   c. The average duration of an outage during a defined period (for example, 1 year)

4. What is an incident?

   a. An event that causes an unexpected result or outage to a business service

   b. An event that has repeatedly caused issues to services and requires some form of root cause analysis

5. Which of the following is a service catalog?

   a. A list of services supported by the IT help desk function in a business

   b. A list of services to be considered in the event of a full DR plan or platform change

   c. Both a and b

6. A service that is designed for high availability should have which of the following?

   a. No single point of failure

   b. Redundancy factors implemented to appropriate levels

   c. No service outage to users

7. In a company that has a virtualize-first strategy, a new application platform is being designed for a critical custom application. Which of the following would prevent the company from virtualizing the application in its entirety?

   a. Vendor support is not available on a virtual platform.

   b. Company compliance requires network and application separation.

   c. Resource profiles are currently unknown and likely to be highly variable.

8. What is RTO?

   a. The maximum amount of time a solution must take to restore a service

   b. The time at which a solution is restored after a failure

9. What is RPO time?

   a. The time at which a solution is restored to after a failure

   b. The maximum amount of time a solution must take to restore a service

10. The IT service desk function is valuable for which of the following?

   a. An operations department, to manage a service catalog and resolve incidents

   b. A technical designer, to measure project success

   c. A technical designer, to obtain requirements

   d. All the above

Foundation Topics

What Makes a Good Choice for Virtualization, and What Is a Good Design?

The VMware vSphere Install, Configure, Manage course teaches that a good choice for virtualization is a "well-behaved application." An application that is badly coded or that has memory or CPU process issues, for example, can behave poorly on a virtual platform even if it performs acceptably on a physical platform.

There may be a few differences between an application running in a physical platform and the same application running in a virtualization platform. One example is the impact on other applications when such problems occur. For example, memory peaks when a Windows service in an application stalls, and this could cause a virtual machine to request more and more memory (up to the amount of configured memory) from the hypervisor. This, in turn, causes host active memory overcommitment and possibly has an application impact, with other workloads not being able to utilize memory as needed on the same physical host.

Creating a good virtual machine guest design, based on the application attributes, to create a well-behaved workload (assuming that the application is stable) is crucial. The specific elements that make up guest design are discussed in Chapter 5, "Virtual Machine Design."

What makes a good design in general, though? You need to answer this question before you can make any specific design choices. Consider a normal enterprise IT platform with file, print, email, and business application services. If the platform hosts the applications so work is generally completed on time, and the company makes money, can the IT platform be classed as a success and also a good design? The answer may be "yes" to some extent, but there are many factors to consider.

Figure 3-1 and Table 3-2 show a key list of considerations an architect should always use to validate designs and plans. These infrastructure qualities are availability, manageability, performance, recoverability, and security. If virtualizing an application affects any of these qualities detrimentally, you need to answer the question "Should I virtualize?" When you're considering vSphere platforms or infrastructure solutions in general, these key aspects are extremely useful as a minimum checklist to ensure that a good, well-thought-out design has been created.

Figure 3-1   General Areas to Consider with the Infrastructure Qualities

Table 3-2   The Infrastructure Qualities

Quality	Description
Availability	The requirements for uptime and whether fault tolerance is required
Manageability	A system that works and doesn't need an army of dedicated engineers
Performance	KPI and satisfaction
Recoverability	How long it takes to recover; how long can the business do without it? How much data loss can be tolerated?
Security	A balance of ease of access and preventing intruders

A platform designer must develop a platform that meets the business objectives or requirements. It can be very easy to see nothing else but the requirements and to produce a solution that, although it meets requirements, is not a technically good design.

Say that a technical consultant has been hired by a business department in a large enterprise to deploy a specific multitier application. The normal in-house IT department performs the enterprise application deployment; however, due to a backlog and internal processes, the delivery time is far longer than the business department can tolerate in current market conditions. The main vision is to deploy a specific application as quickly as possible. It consists of three tiers:

- Web tier

- Application tier

- Database tier

The application vendor can provide support in the event of a development issue.

The business department has several projects to place in this application, within a very tight time frame.

The technical consultant reviews the size of the current project workload and considers the minimum specifications for the software:

- One small server for the web tier

- One small server for the application tier

- One medium server with an attached local disk array for the database tier

A project plan is constructed to deploy the application, hardware is acquired, and the platform is built for around $30,000. Approximately seven days after the consultant begins work, the application is in production, and the business department is using the application on live projects.

Has the project been a success? It depends. What are the expectations from the business? The application is in production; it is serving the current workloads, and both the business users and end clients are happy. The project has technically met business requirements. However, consider a few scenarios:

- What if the web server operating system crashes?

- What if the workloads increase dramatically?

- What if a security patch needs to be installed?

- What if the hardware fails?

- What if the system is hacked?
- What if there is a human error, and the data is deleted with a SQL job or a remote access query?

Would the business reasonably consider that the application should be tolerant to these issues? A customer or client may not specify these kinds of things, but a platform designer should at least consider them. It is assumed that the technical requirements discussed during interviews during the information gathering phase would have identified the expectations.

When you factor in these possible issues, the delivery time frame may be unsuitable for the business, or the cost may be too much for the current projects. However, the project team should be made aware that there are possible associated risks with the proposed design and the current technical approach. All these scenarios could be stated as assumptions or risks (for example, "It is assumed that the business does not require disaster recovery").

If the business takes on more projects that use this application, or if the criticality of the data changes (for example, through brand damage), a subsequent project could be created to add the ability to scale or recover. Should ease of scalability be considered in the original installation, or does the business feel comfortable with a quick installation, going live, seeing if it works and sells, and repeating with a bigger project, considering the possible scenarios that might affect the infrastructure?

When a platform or VMware designer is asked to review or to plan a solution, it is crucial that with all the technical platform components, the designer considers the attributes of good design—whether they are specifically requested or not. These attributes may not change an approach in some cases, but in others they could prevent a possible project failure. A platform designer must show due diligence and ensure that every design is of a good quality as well as functional for the end client.

Personally, I use the infrastructure qualities as a checklist. Each quality helps form a set of questions and areas to consider while I'm designing or reviewing a design. If I can check each quality as considered and incorporated in the design, I feel more comfortable.

The key thoughts associated with each quality will differ from project to project. Figure 3-1 shows some of the general areas to consider.

"It's Okay, We Have HA!"

This is a statement I have heard in many meetings. It is sometimes valid, depending on the business requirements. But before it can be taken as true, a VMware architect needs to clarify a few basic points:

- How long the business can be without the service

- What state the system needs to be in once it is restored

- Cost expectations

RTO, RPO, and All That Stuff

Nothing can make a techie switch off quicker than the mention of acronyms such as RTO and RPO. However, these aspects are pretty crucial to a designer.

The *recovery time objective* (RTO)—also known as the *return to operation*—is the amount of time it takes to restore a service after a failure has taken place. The *recovery point objective* (RPO) is the point in time to which the system needs to be restored following a failure.

Say that a database crashes at 1 a.m. on Sunday morning. The website is rendered unusable. Users cannot log into their accounts. The company has a service-level agreement (SLA) with an RTO of 4 hours and an RPO of 15 minutes.

The design for the solution must provide a system that can be completely restored within 4 hours of the outage (that is, the RTO). Within 4 hours, the system must also be in the state it was in at a maximum of 15 minutes before the outage (that is, the RPO).

The RTO and RPO expectations can have a dramatic effect on the other infrastructure qualities. The lower these values, the less time the business can tolerate the service being unavailable. Added redundancy may be required. But additional redundancy can add complexity, which may in turn reduce the ease of management or in some cases make the platform harder to secure.

Understanding an application's data flow is extremely useful. Consider the following scenario: You are a VMware consultant at a web firm. The latest solution consists of a multitier application. There are three major server roles:

- Web server—Provides web content with IIS and a custom application service.

- Application servers—Provides a platform for three services:
    - Listener service that takes data from a UDP feed
    - Integration service to an application
    - Calculation service

- Database—Provides a large single instance of Microsoft SQL 2008

The application listener service takes relevant data from the feed and places it in an in-memory database. The calculation service takes this useful data and places it into usable form in the database. The web service communicates with the database and provides data to the user.

The SLA specifies an RTO of 4 hours and an RPO of 15 minutes.

From a platform perspective, a well-thought-out and configured HA solution combined with a backup/restore routine could in fact meet the SLA. Closer inspection is needed, however.

VMware HA handles a host or virtual machine restart in an automated way. The fact that the system has a number of services and an in-memory database raises concerns about usability and the state of the servers in the event of a restart. Do the services restart automatically? How long does it take for the in-memory database to populate and display to the end user? The answers to these questions will help the designer determine whether HA meets the requirements. In my experience, the RTO of a few minutes using VMware HA is enough for the majority of business applications.

Ultimately, it is the end users' experience that matters. End users expect their systems to work and their data to be available when needed. But what does "when needed" mean?

Consider a multitier application. The end users review data over a web connection; internal analysts upload and process data from a backend private connection. Who are the end users? From an infrastructure perspective, different levels of availability may be required for the two sets of users: An SLA helps for service delivery, but when designing a platform, it would be beneficial to understand the working practices.

In this example, the different user types at each end of the product life cycle could make your application uptime requirement a lot higher than expected. This concern would not only need to be addressed in a solution but brought to the attention of management if solutions are impractical in regard to costs and so on.

Single Points of Failure and Risk

Many IT engineers look at a technology and highlight the obvious single points of failure. This is a good practice, but it's important to also answer some follow-up questions:

- How likely is it that this failure will happen, and are the improvements required to remove all single points of failure pragmatic from a business standpoint?

- What do we gain by removing the single points of failure?

- What about factors such as cost and ease of support and complexity? What about the applications running on or using the platform?

Consider another scenario, in which internal users use an application to upload large amounts of data using an application-specific upload tool. As part of the upload process, this tool removes file extensions and changes file names to globally unique identifiers (GUIDs). The removed information is pushed into a load file and placed into a database.

End users log in to a website and review the uploaded data securely by searching the database and being presented with rendered images of the documents. No sensitive file names or executables are revealed to the outside world. A high level of availability is required in this case. The RTO is 4 hours, and RPO is 1 day.

A platform architect could start to build in HA by using mirrored databases and multiple single-port cards throughout. He could present a detailed process to allow the operations guys to back up and restore the individual components.

A full disaster recovery test, often neglected until later in the project, can expose a number of issues. In this example, the operations team restores all servers from backups and templates, and all are individually successful. Great news!

The issue that arises is that the original data is backed up and restored, but the uploaded data from the tool is not backed up and restored. The team determines that the data needs to be uploaded to the remote hosting site and the original native form should be suitable.

The database is restored, and it contains a list of GUIDs that reference documents. The original data is uploaded using the tool and given different GUIDs. This process makes the application unusable, and the objective of bringing the service back fails within the time frame of the SLA. It is possible to add remedial steps such as backing up the uploaded data and contacting the vendor to repopulate GUIDs in a restore mode. These measures would fail to work in the SLA time frame with the platform that has been designed.

Although such a restore problem may be difficult for a platform engineer to spot, this issue could have a major impact on a business. In this example, is the process a complete failure? Not at all. The tested process could in fact meet business continuity requirements. The application consists of 20+ servers; the likelihood of all servers being corrupted or impacted in the designed stable environment is very low. Therefore, a more likely request would be to restore a specific server. A file server with static data could be seen as a low risk.

This example illustrates the difference between planning for handling problems while keeping the system up and running with some user impact (for example, one project down versus all projects down) and planning to recover from a major outage.

What Is DR, and When Is It Invoked?

In the example we've been looking at, it is understood that due to how the application works and factors such as security of the documents, the recovery of the full system could take a long time. Defining when the DR process (that is, full restore of service to RTO and RPO times) should be invoked would therefore be useful. For instance, a single project corruption caused by a server error may not necessarily cause the DR process to be invoked. The impact to the other projects outweighs the loss of data in that one project.

Defining clear entry criteria and success criteria for DR would make these times less stressful. Who will perform the DR process? How complicated is the process of DR? Having a DR plan that encompasses the items listed here would ensure that in the event of an emergency, the service can be brought back in a clear, methodical manner:

- Entity relationship diagram
- Key contacts in the business and vendor support
- End user notification process
- Information on backup strategy and location
- Entry criteria for the DR process
- Operations guide on the service restore process
- How to determine whether the service is successful

Testing the DR process for a service is normally carried out a specified minimum number of times per year. A platform architect should consider a well-tested and verified DR process critical and a key factor in the measurement of a successful project finish.

Platform and Operations: The Roles

Business as usual (BAU) is a term that an aspiring senior engineer or consultant dreads. After several years of backups, archiving, and solving user queries, the excitement tends to drop. Enter the platform role: looking at new products and working on projects that can have a great impact on the business and the users.

BAU experience is invaluable, and as part of any consultancy project I find it a good benchmark on how well the project has run. Proper project scoping and implementation make a solution easy to support. So does understanding regular processes and, where possible, documenting them. If a solution goes live and your help desk is suddenly alive with calls, maybe you need to have another look at the implementation or design.

In a recent contract, I took the role of an IT consultant working directly for a business department. I was not a member of the IT team. In fact, from their perspective, I was just another user and someone to watch with regard to projects. The business had unique needs that the current service was not designed to support. The users wanted results—quickly and with a high level of quality. Having a direct relationship with users gave me an advantage in understanding their applications, user processes, and so on, and the projects started to have a great impact.

As things developed, the finished solutions required support and monitoring. New projects came along, and with them came the need for more staff and processes with which to manage them. One of these new guys was an individual with limited experience in IT who possessed some skills from various applications and certifications but had no knowledge of the specific environment. What did that person need in order to understand the new role and support the environment? Documentation? Team shadowing? Being able to sink or swim with the systems?

It was time to create a standard IT function. However, the new requirement to fill in tickets, raise requests, or ask for updates via official routes was not what the users wanted. They expected the same service they had been getting from the beginning.

The help desk function can be more useful to IT and the architect than to the end user. Most help desk systems have a list of applications from which the user should select when raising an incident. By listing these services and applications, and then defining a suitable response and fix time, you actually create a service catalog. This catalog is not only valuable to the help desk but also as a review of systems used by the business—a snapshot of what is needed in the event of a failure. This catalog contains all manner of important information.

I always request access to the help desk system. Reviewing the recurring calls can be valuable when you're assessing how well a system is performing, and it yields a list of key requirements that can be addressed so that users feel rapid improvement. These items could also be publicized in release documentation or presentations before a project or an upgrade goes live.

"Did Someone Change Something on Production?"

This is a scary question, but it's a very common one, especially with the speed of deployment that VMware platforms can bring to a business and the resultant user expectation for rapid delivery. There is increasing pressure to just get things done.

The introduction of change management can seem painful for a team that has never really used it. Phrases such as "I'm only making a simple change," "It will be fine," and "It's been done before" are sure to pop up.

Change management is a good thing for IT staff. It allows a change to be well thought out, with all aspects considered. However, it is a balancing act. A change management system is there to ensure quality and planned changes with minimum impact. It is all too easy to create a change management system that is either too complicated or too long winded to navigate.

In creating a change management system, it's important to consider the main components of a request for change:

- A change summary

- Impact

- Change process

- Rollback procedure

- Verification process

- Information on the person making the change and the time of the change

- Approval status

Who approves the change? Ideally, a change advisory board should consist of business and technical staff. The board should be able to discuss risks, the impact to the application service, and technical aspects.

Figure 3-2 shows an example of a change request form, with considerations for rollback, risks, and implementation.

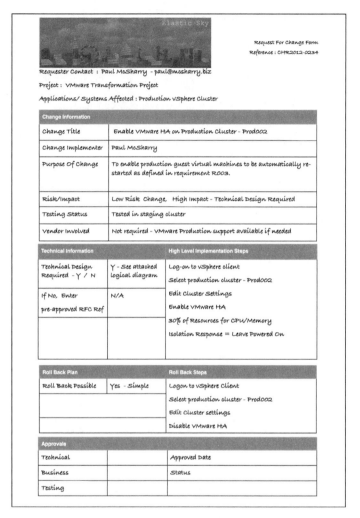

Figure 3-2 An Example of a Change Request Form

When to Virtualize?

On a recent project, a custom Windows application was developed within a VMware-hosted platform. The developer's machine had one vCPU assigned to it. The application essentially took numbers from a feed, opened up the the filtered data in Excel, which contained a calculation, and then exported the results to a database.

This system made its way through the software development life cycle (SDLC). Due to the number of calculations envisioned at peak times, the management decided that this system would require dedicated physical hardware. After it was installed on the live hardware, the application crashed after 2 or 3 seconds of use.

Redeploying the application to a virtual copy worked. However, adding more vCPUs to the one vCPU box and restarting caused the system to crash in a matter of seconds. Reducing them down to two vCPUs resulted in several minutes of up-time. When put back to one vCPU, the application was stable again.

After a more in-depth look at the issue, it was discovered that because Excel was intended for a single user or terminal service access, this highly transactional nature of opening and closing Excel was not supported and not stable. The solution? Install ESXi on the powerful physical boxes and deploy lots of smaller one-vCPU application servers.

In this example, the business's preference was originally for a physical deployment rather than a virtual platform. However, after running into problems, it was determined that the less costly option was to deploy to a virtual platform rather than to redevelop the application.

For a virtualization architect, the question of whether to virtualize could be seen as a ridiculous one. When can you *not* virtualize? Wasted resources and deploying on a platform less flexible than a VMware platform could seem like bad design practices.

Various factors can influence the decision of whether to virtualize, including the following:

- **Application**—Is it supported on a virtualized platform?
- **Licensing costs**—They are unfriendly to a virtualized platform.
- **Compliance**—Air space is required between systems and cannot be shared (even with the hypervisor).
- **Support is too complex**—Virtualization skills can add cost.

From a design perspective, if the application requirements can be met and the infrastructure qualities can be considered, virtualization is a good choice for most systems. For specific information on what to consider when virtualizing an application, see Chapter 5.

Exam Preparation Tasks

Review All Key Topics

Review the most important topics in the chapter, noted with the key topics icon in the outer margin of the page. Table 3-3 lists these key topics and the page number on which each is found.

Table 3-3   Key Topics

Key Topic Element	Description	Page
Table 3-2 and Figure 3-1	The infrastructure qualities	39
List	The DR plan and process	45
Paragraph	Did someone change something on production?	47

Design Scenario

You are a virtualization consultant working in a business department. You have been tasked with virtualizing an existing multitier application. The current platform is hosted on physical hardware.

The application has three server roles:

- Web server
- Application server
- Database server

You have attended a kickoff meeting with the CTO and the operations manager. The following were key points in the meeting:

- The system is not performing as required by the business for current loads.
- The number of projects will double within 3 months.
- The vendor has not virtualized this system before, but the vendor has dedicated time with your client to work to complete this process successfully.

- The business is now shifting all production work to this vendor solution, and the SLA has changed and now looks like this:
  - Uptime: 99.9% per year
  - RTO: 4 hours
  - RPO: 15 minutes

Complete these tasks:

1. Draw a logical diagram of the server roles.

2. Add access points to the diagram.

3. Write out the infrastructure qualities and add at least three key points for consideration on moving this application to a virtualized platform. What information do you require, and what key questions can help you get it?

4. Recommend a possible solution and draw a logical diagram.

5. Make a bulleted list of how this solution meets the businesses need.

6. Consider and list the daily tasks or daily checks that would need to be carried out on the proposed platform by the operations team (for example, patching, hardware maintenance).

7. Consider a DR plan based on the RTO and RPO requirements listed.

As part of these tasks, you do the following:

- Create a high-level logical diagram
- Consider infrastructure qualities during a design process
- Introduce operational practices from a logical design
- Create a DR plan based on requirements
- Consider continuous improvement by recommending changes on a new design

These aspects are heavily tested and assumed in the VCAP5-DCD exam.

Definitions of Key Terms

Define the following key terms from this chapter and check your answers in the glossary.

Recovery time objective (RTO), Recovery point objective (RPO), Mean time between failures (MTBF), Service Asset and Configuration Management (CMDB) system, Capacity plan

Review Questions

The answers to these review questions are in Appendix A.

1. Which of the following is a list of attributes that can be used as a checklist for ensuring good design thoughts?

    a. The project requirements

    b. The infrastructure qualities

    c. The project design choices

2. Which of the following could prevent a physical system from being converted to a virtual workload?

    a. The physical system uses legacy operating systems, such as Windows NT 4.

    b. The application running on the physical server is not supported in a virtual platform.

    c. The application has not been tested in a virtual platform.

3. The infrastructure qualities are attributes you can use to ensure that major aspects are considered to help with good design processes. What are the infrastructure qualities?

    a. RTO, RPO, and MTBF

    b. Availability, manageability, performance, recoverability, and security

    c. Capacity, change control, security, DR, and supportability

4. A platform has an RPO of 4 hours. The platform crashes at 2 p.m. Which of the following is correct?

    a. The platform must be ready for users to access by 6 p.m., with data versions from at least from 10 a.m.

    b. The platform must be ready for users ASAP, with data versions from at least 10 a.m.

    c. The platform must be ready for users to access by 6 p.m., and the data age is unknown from the RTO.

5. A multitier website has an RTO of 4 hours and an RPO of 15 minutes. The database crashes at 5 p.m. and causes the website to be unavailable. Which of the following is true? (Select all that apply.)

   a. The website must be restored by 5:15 p.m.

   b. The website must be restored by 9 p.m.

   c. At restore time, the data must be correct from at least from 4:45 p.m.

   d. At restore time, the data must be from at least 1 p.m.

6. You are the VMware consultant at a large enterprise. A senior manager is in charge of a project that needs new infrastructure for its application. The application will be used by 3,200 users. Three virtual machines are requested via the help desk. One of the three is a virtual machine with 32 vCPUs allocated for processing. The notes of the request say that the large number of vCPUs (the company template is 2 vCPUs) is justified by the senior manager. The notes also reference the following details from the application manual:

   ■ For every 100 users in the workload, the processing tier of the application requires one agent handler service.

   ■ Each agent handler requires one single-core CPU.

   Which of the following should the VMware consultant do next?

   a. Configure the 32-vCPU box as requested and talk to the users during the rest of the project to understand the application as much as possible for ease of support and to understand the impact.

   b. Create a proof of concept server with 2 vCPUs and engage with the user/application vendor to understand actual resources required for the company workload and support requirements. Suggest other deployment strategies, such as scaling out the processing tier with a lower number of vCPUs per guest virtual machine but more virtual machines within the tier.

   c. Deny the virtual machine request and suggest that the processing tier be physical.

This chapter covers the following subjects:

- **How to Approach vSphere Technical Design:** This section explains what to consider when designing a platform from each type of vSphere component: compute, network, storage, and management.

- **Design Thoughts, Choices, and Impact Considerations:** This section discusses how design choices can impact a solution and the mindset a designer needs to adopt.

- **The Importance of vMotion, VMware HA, and Fault Tolerance:** This section covers how the availability and performance features of vSphere can impact a design.

This chapter covers the following objectives of the VCAP5-DCD blueprint:

- Objective 3.1, "Transition from a logical design to a vSphere 5 physical design"

- Objective 3.2, "Create a vSphere 5 physical network design from an existing logical design"

- Objective 3.3, "Create a vSphere 5 physical storage design from an existing logical design"

- Objective 3.4, "Determine appropriate compute resources for a vSphere 5 physical design"

- Objective 3.6, "Determine datacenter management options for a vSphere 5 physical design"

CHAPTER 4

Developing a Design on Paper and Delivering It Physically

Developing an understanding of a business problem and how an IT solution can be either the root cause or can be improved or used to solve a business problem is a very useful skill. vSphere platforms consist of compute, network, storage, and management components. If you gather information discussed in Chapters 2, "Creating a Design," and 3, "Thoughts on Good Choices for Virtualization and Design," and develop a logical design for each of these components, the physical or real-life deliverable should meet user expectations.

"Do I Know This Already?" Quiz

The "Do I Know This Already?" quiz allows you to assess whether you should read this entire chapter or simply jump to the "Exam Preparation Tasks" section for review. If you are in doubt, read the entire chapter. Table 4-1 outlines the major headings in this chapter and the corresponding "Do I Know This Already?" quiz questions. You can find the answers in Appendix A, "Answers to the 'Do I Know This Already?' and Chapter Review Questions."

Table 4-1 "Do I Know This Already?" Foundation Topics Section-to-Question Mapping

Foundations Topics Section	Questions Covered in This Section
How to Approach vSphere Technical Design	1–3, 11, 14, 15
Design Thoughts, Choices, and Impact Considerations	4, 6, 8, 9
The Importance of VMotion, VMware HA, and Fault Tolerance	5, 7, 10, 12, 13

1. Which of the following can determine the maximum datastore size?

   a. The RTO SLA of the data

   b. The size of the largest guest virtual machine plus the size of the swap file

2. Storage tiering can be used to create a life cycle of data from its business-critical point on highly performant storage to nearly archival on cheaper, bigger, less performant disks.

   a. True

   b. False

3. Which of the following can determine the minimum datastore size?

   a. The RTO SLA of the data

   b. The size of the largest guest virtual machine plus the size of the swap file

   c. The RPO SLA of the data

4. You develop a physical storage design before you develop a logical design.

   a. True

   b. False

5. Which of the following is not a vSphere component to consider from a design perspective?

   a. Storage layer component

   b. Network layer component

   c. Availability layer component

   d. Compute layer component

   e. Management layer component

6. Best practices are higher priority than project requirements for implementation.

   a. True

   b. False

7. An enterprise has three tiers of storage:

Storage Tier	High-Level Details
Gold	Highest performance, SSD disks
Silver	SAS, 15000 RPM, RAID 1
Bronze	SATA, 7200 RPM, RAID 5

Which of the following statements is true?

  a. Storage vMotion, Storage DRS, and Profile-Driven Storage vSphere technologies could decrease the total storage capacity required by the business.

  b. Storage vMotion, Storage DRS, and Profile-Driven Storage vSphere technologies could decrease the amount of Gold and Silver storage required by migrating workloads with different peak usage times.

8. Best practices can help guide a physical design, as long as project requirements are met.

  a. True

  b. False

9. Your platform has seven datastores; each of them has a dedicated allocation of disks. A gold master virtual template has been deployed 20 times to each datastore, and a variety of different software has been installed on them. All datastores except one are satisfying workload SLA requirements. It appears that a single application server is consuming 70% of the I/O on the problem datastore. Which of the following would be the most appropriate solution in this case?

  a. Enable Storage I/O Control, subject to other project requirements not being impacted.

  b. Create a new datastore specifically for the application server and migrate the application server using Storage vMotion. This would ensure that other vSphere components are not impacted.

  c. Create a Storage DRS anti-affinity rule to prevent the I/O-intensive server from running in the datastore with high latency.

10. From a design perspective, when should guest thin provisioning be used?

   a. When there is a limited amount of datastore space for the guests on the datastore

   b. When the guest VM's disk capacity usage is fixed

   c. When the guest VM's disk capacity usage is variable, with a low IOPS requirement

11. Which of the following information gathering methods is most accurate in creating a storage design?

   a. An active discovery-based tool

   b. A vendor- or load-based calculation tool

12. What determines the RTO and RPO of a storage platform?

   a. The datastore size

   b. The vendor guidelines

   c. The business requirements

13. You are a VMware designer at a large enterprise. The production project you are working on requires a vSphere 5 datastore design. After discussing the project with the platform team, what is the maximum datastore size achievable without further investment in operational procedures, assuming that the following information is true: All production data requires an RTO of 3 hours, and the backup service can restore 1 TB per hour.

   a. 2 TB – 512kb

   b. 2 TB

   c. 64 TB in a single extent

   d. 3 TB

14. Which of the following does a physical design include?

   a. High-level components and how they relate to the solution

   b. Detailed information regarding the components, such as model of systems, IP addresses, and configurations

15. When transitioning from a logical design to a physical design, you have a choice of using one of several solutions. Which of the following should you always consider?

    a. Project requirements

    b. Cost of implementation

    c. Existing vendor relationship

Foundation Topics

How to Approach vSphere Technical Design

Until this point, we have discussed what a design methodology is and why it is important to follow one. How does this apply to vSphere design, and what should be considered specifically for VMware platforms?

Having the following thoughts in mind when working to a design methodology on a vSphere platform project can help you make good design choices:

- It's all about the application or workload!
    - What is the function of the application?
    - Who is the user?
    - How does the application work, and how does data flow between servers/systems?
    - Is the workload CPU bound or memory bound or both?
    - Is the application single-tier or multitier?

- What is the best practice, and should I use it?
    - Vendor- and community-based best practices should be considered and justified, if used.
    - Best practices should be based on successful experience with the technology, thus saving time and producing a high-quality design.
    - Best practices should not conflict with project requirements.

- Consider the infrastructure qualities throughout the design process: availability, manageability, performance, recoverability, and security.
- Costs and value:
    - Can all the design factors be justified?
    - Designing a system can be a balancing act between a multitude of design factors.

The key aim is to produce a stable and secure platform for the applications to achieve their SLA.

Best practices and ease of management mean very little to users; they are not requirements but may help guide you toward design choices in the absence of absolute requirements.

Transitioning to a Physical Design: A Common Approach and Process

Designing a vSphere platform from the ground up can seem a very complicated task. One process that has worked for me in the real world is to look at the platform components and apply a common approach. Here's one way to do it:

1. Create a conceptual design for the project. Illustrate how this idea will solve the business problem or create a stable platform for user workloads.

2. From this concept, develop a logical design for each component, based on project functional requirements, incorporating factors such as risks, constraints, and assumptions agreed from the project spec or information gathering stage.

3. Consider best practices from the community or vendors.

4. Check the infrastructure qualities. Doing so will allow you to validate your logical design.

I recommend reviewing your designs with the rest of the project team and the business sponsors or stakeholders. Walk through the solution and illustrate how the requirements are met and how the infrastructure qualities validate your choices. Ensure that you can justify each choice and understand the impact each one has. It would be highly advisable to have sign-off from others at this stage, as it is early enough in the overall process to make changes without substantial costs and time wastage.

From the approved logical design, you can consider actual solutions and create a physical design to implement in real life. A logical design is independent of hardware, while a physical design has vendor components and specific technology (and other aspects, too, such as part numbers and IP addresses specified).

For example, in a vSphere storage design, lots of vendors (for example, NetApp, HP) have fantastic solutions. Your general platform knowledge or research techniques will come into play here. You need to make an informed decision on behalf of the business, so do the following:

- Talk to vendors.

- Talk to the community.

- Leverage existing relationships with vendors and colleagues for support.

- Read about the subjects, look at case studies, and ask for references.

For each proposed implementation of the logical design, do the following:

- Confirm that the project requirements are all met.

- Again check the infrastructure qualities for design validation.

- Compare against other factors, such as cost/budget and possible impact to other parts of the datacenter, if implemented.

When you implement one technology, consider whether it might have a detrimental effect on another technology already implemented in the business. One example I have come across is the use of VDI—a fantastic technology and business enabler. Placing all users' work on virtual desktops running in the datacenter would be beneficial. One project I was leading from a VMware perspective, however, aimed to consolidate as many servers as possible and upgrade to Windows 7 VDI desktops from normal thick desktops running Windows XP, allowing all users to work from any location.

The current network link to the datacenter was not designed for this level of additional traffic; it was implemented 2 years prior to this project, and the company was tied to a special contract for 5 years. In addition, the VPN device to allow users to work from home from this datacenter was not designed for mass use of VDI but for administrative remote desktop access in case of emergency. Implementing VDI without looking for such issues could have led to project failure, loss of confidence, and a lot of wasted time and money for the business.

Normally as part of a solution design, I include three possible physical design options (consisting of various implementations of technology to meet the logical design). These design options can be developed for various reasons, such as the following:

- **Costs**—Cheap, midrange, or best of breed

- **Speed of implementation**—Quick and functional, mid-term (functional and easy to support), or strategic (can be reused for other projects as a model of implementation)

- **Least impact (for example, in a datacenter migration)**—Big bang (just lift and shift everything over a weekend), gradual (lift and shift service-by-service, with the least impact first so you can understand the impact and gain experience), or seamless cutover (make datacenter B production and datacenter A the DR; flip between the two without an outage for any specific applications)

vSphere Platform Components

From a design perspective, the vSphere platform consists of five components, all of which are highly linked. Good design is needed to aggregate these five components into a stable and scalable platform (see Figure 4-1):

- The storage layer

- The network layer

- The compute layer

- The guest VM layer (discussed in Chapter 5, "Virtual Machine Design")

- The management layer

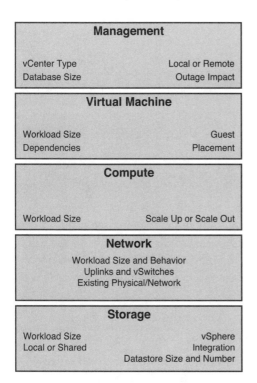

Figure 4-1   vSphere Platform Components

The VCAP5-DCD exam looks at each of these layers in regard to creating a logical and physical design. It is possible to take each component in turn and study the technology in fine detail. The information you glean by doing so is extremely valuable and useful for real-life implementations.

However, the role of a VMware designer/architect is to create a platform using these component layers and to satisfy the business requirements while understanding VMware technology and general datacenter information. It is this design skill that the VCAP-DCD5 exam tests.

Design Thoughts, Choices, and Impact Considerations

The following sections briefly examine each of the vSphere component layers (see Figure 4-2), highlight a process to help in the design of this component, and discuss some design choices and their possible impacts. This section is not exhaustive by any means, but provides an example on how to dismantle each component and how to discuss some important design factors.

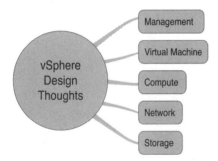

Figure 4-2   vSphere Design Thoughts—High Level

The main purpose of this section is to get you thinking in the mindset of the VCAP5-DCD exam and hopefully also use these principles in real life. As you will see, this chapter highlights common issues and suggests processes, but this is not a full guide for all logical and physical solutions; it is meant to guide you toward creating your own.

Storage Design: Logical and Physical Approaches

Whether in the physical world or the virtual world, applications can read or write data. Depending on the type of application and its processes, the amount of read or write actions will vary.

It is the role of the underlying platform to provide an application with the ability to write or read data when the application requires it. As data is the start and end of most processes in applications, it can be the most valuable asset to a business. In addition to being able to read and write data effectively, a platform must also protect data from possible corruption, and it must ensure that only the users authorized to access the data can do so.

In the physical deployed world, where operating systems are physically bound to their hardware, systems have local storage and dedicated disks. To ensure that read and write times are acceptable, the data may be spread across multiple disks (spindles), and multiple copies may exist for concurrent reads or to mitigate against corruption.

In the virtual world, the application requirements are the same. The functions of the applications don't change, but the mode of the storage delivery does. By consolidating workloads onto fewer physical servers and moving to a shared centralized storage network, an IT professional must ensure (with the amount of capacity available) that all the workloads get the required number of read/write operations to perform the function to the SLA that the user expects.

From a VMware platform design perspective, vSphere is storage agnostic. The software can be configured to create a scalable and stable production platform. Logically, there are two main types:

- Local storage with vSphere
- Shared storage with vSphere

Local Storage with vSphere

Data is bound to the local device, and this could prevent management or maintenance if the SLA has aggressive uptime requirements. (However, with the release of vSphere 5.1, Enhanced vMotion can be used to migrate these workloads manually.)

Scalability could be affected by the number of slots in the physical unit. In fact, this constraint could also increase the cost of a server unit to support the amount of storage.

Dedicated storage ensures that an application will have complete access to the appropriate amount of I/O and does not need to compete with other applications. This may initially be perfect, but if the demands increase, there is still only a fixed level of resource. How can it scale? Will there be an outage if required to scale for larger demands of I/O or amount of data?

Shared Storage with vSphere

Workloads can be moved from a storage type or level while still being actively used by end users, both for maintenance and to balance application I/O requirements. This feature (called Storage DRS) allows the possibility of using smaller amounts of storage but a wider variety of tiers. Used intelligently, this could provide a better level of service: All systems at the critical point in the life cycle could be provided the highest level of storage.

In the event of a host outage, the data can be accessed on other hosts, and workloads can be restarted, thereby removing dependency on a single piece of hardware or the need for the business to buy multiple pieces of hardware with low return on investment. For example, paying for an identical server as a restore point would involve a server being deployed, powered, and managed as if it were in production—but for very little usage.

Storage Tiering

Storage tiering is a management technique whereby different types of storage that fulfill different SLAs can be implemented.

Data is managed via a life cycle approach from creation to most critical and ultimately to archival. The data is migrated (seamlessly, thanks to today's technology) and placed on different levels of storage, depending where it is in the life cycle.

A real-life example of this is an IT security firm working on a possibly compromised platform. The IT firm sends an analyst to gather as much information as possible (that is, terabytes and terabytes of storage) and bring it back into the investigation platform for examination. Here the data is processed, with an experienced security professional looking for traces of suspicious activity. After that check, it can then be presented in a suitable way for client review.

From a storage platform perspective, these are the main points in the life cycle in this example:

- **Data acquisition**—The original data is copied from the client.

- **Data processing**—The client data is copied and examined for activity (which can take many person hours).

- **Data review**—The data is parceled up for review by the client.

- **Archival**—The data can be requested for a period of time, which varies from project to project (for example, 1, 2, 5, or 7 years). The archival stage is not required immediately after the review.

An IT security firm has multiple projects and clients at one time. The in-house storage admin would have an unsustainable job without tiering (unless the budget for buying more storage, space, power, and so on were limitless); the amount of data will just increase.

In this example, as shown in Table 4-2, storage tiers could be created based on the process:

- **Type III**—The client data copied to the IT security firm will never change. As data is copied for processing, this version could be placed on large, cheaper storage, which remains available until all data has been processed or is under review.

- **Type II**—This is a highly important tier of storage. The processed data represents many hours of work for the team. However, original data is still available in the event of a disaster. One backup strategy could be a SAN-based snapshot, kept for 2 to 4 weeks. If older than 2 weeks, the data could be recovered from Tier III and reprocessed. Type II data could demand high read and write I/O and needs a good level of protection, such as RAID 1+0. However, due to the size and cost of disks, RAID 5 could be acceptable for providing access to storage with some redundancy. The impact in the event of disk failures would be internal-only performance.

- **Type I**—This is the most critical tier of storage. In this example, client review and acceptance represent many hours of work. Therefore, this tier should feature faster disks and the ability to review data even in the event of a disk failure.

Table 4-2 A Storage Tier Specifications Example

Storage Tier Name	Level	Type of Disk	Number of Disks	RAID
Type I	Critical	SSD	120	1+0
Type II	Normal	SAS	240	5
Type III	Low	SATA	480	5

When you understand the business processes and create storage tiers, the project data can move between the layers from data acquisition (Type III), through to processing (Type II or I), client review (Type I), and to archival (Type III). Ultimately, when a project closes down, the original data and review data can be archived for the required retention time.

This real-life problem and basic solution illustrates the thoughts and basic high-level process a vSphere designer needs to follow to support virtual workloads:

1. Understand the business problem and processes.

2. Understand the workload requirements.

3. Create a conceptual logical design (see Figures 4-3 and 4-4).

4. Create a physical design with components that can satisfy the logical design, taking into consideration other variables (for example, costs).

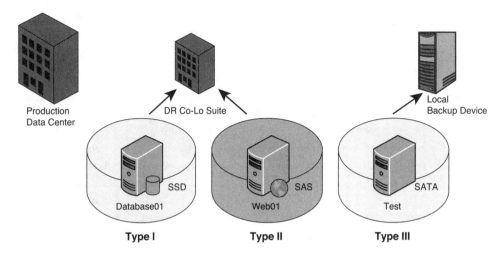

Figure 4-3   Conceptual Logical Diagram of a Storage Design

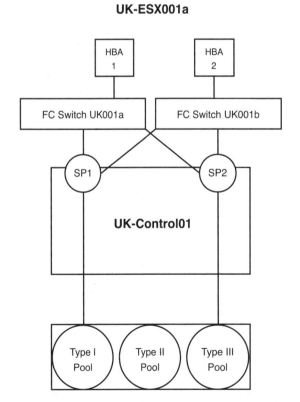

Figure 4-4   High-Level Physical Diagram of a Storage Solution

vSphere Storage Design Decisions

A vSphere admin needs to understand the same requirements as a physical platform designer. In addition, a vSphere admin should consider some "vThoughts," as detailed in Figure 4-5.

Figure 4-5   Design Choices for the Storage Component of vSphere Platforms

A vSphere admin needs to understand some key metrics:

- The amount of IOPS needed at peak and normal working levels (discovery phase).

- The total data capacity

- Throughput (for example, speed of transfer)

- Growth requirements

- SLA

By understanding these metrics, a vSphere admin can create a storage platform that does the following:

- It is correctly sized as a total unit, taking into account growth over a period of time.

- It provides correct performance at the required time of the day. For example, various apps can have different requirements over a 24-hour period. Therefore, the same amount of central storage is required, but maybe a section of slower and cheaper but bigger disks are required as applications can be migrated during peak periods.

- It meets uptime, corruption, and security mitigation; for example, a single storage network endpoint can be linked to another endpoint at another geographic location where data is replicated.

Design Approaches and Development

A VMware designer normally creates a storage design by communicating with a storage vendor or a number of storage professionals. A VCAP-level vSphere designer needs to know what information to provide and what questions to ask the business and the storage experts to enable them to produce a vSphere system that works.

These could be the steps of the design approach:

1. Create a conceptual high-level design from business requirements (for example, whether there are multiple tiers of storage, replication, different SLAs).

2. Develop the conceptual design to a more detailed logical design, using chosen technologies and information from the requirements (either business or derived from workloads).

3. Develop a physical design based on logical design, best practices, and other design factors or dependencies.

A datastore logical design is an important deliverable. It describes how the storage delivered to the ESXi hosts will be carved up and presented to the vSphere environment.

A vSphere designer devises a logical design following a mixture of considerations, including the number of datastores and the size of datastores. How do you calculate the appropriate size and number of datastores? At a basic level, you require storage to hold the project-defined workloads. In the information gathering phase, you confirm the maximum and minimum VM sizes for the workloads you are going to host on the platform. Remember to consider the size and location of the swap file. This is, by default, in the same datastore as the VM, and it is equal to the amount of configured memory minus the memory reservation. This will give you the minimum size of your datastore. Consider adding space for the following:

- Snapshots

- Gradual growth

- Scratch space for movement between datastores

From this calculated figure, the next decision is whether to configure lots of smaller datastores or a smaller number of larger datastores. One factor to weigh up at this point is ease of management. For example, it can be easier to manage a smaller number of larger datastores and implement backup policies and archival processes. Another consideration is the I/O profile of the application. Should you keep highly read applications together or mix them with applications with a higher proportion of writes? This depends on a multitude of factors that can be unique to the use case. It is important at the logical storage design phase to ensure that these requirements are progressed to the physical design so that a suitable storage solution is selected.

The use of VMware technology with Storage DRS, Profile-Driven Storage, and Storage I/O Control (SIOC) available can enable a designer to create larger datastores and rely on per-VM policies to ensure that I/O requirements are met.

Developing a Physical Storage Design

A logical design gives a designer a great deal of knowledge. In my experience, it has been extremely difficult to go straight to a physical solution without going through the design process.

Storage can be very expensive, so if you just go out and buy a piece of hardware, how do you know it is correct? How do you justify the decision? You need to research options for the business. Remember that logical designs are independent of hardware choice. If they are adequately researched and implemented as intended, your choice shouldn't matter. More importantly, the virtual workloads and end users shouldn't care who provides the storage; it just read/writes after all.

One method I use to ensure that I complete my due diligence for storage design is to arm myself with all the information I need to explain to the storage vendor salesperson what I need the hardware to do. I have some clear information and a diagram to show that I clearly know what I require. This saves time for the business, the vendor, and me.

The information you need is likely to vary from project to project. In general, you need to have answers to the following questions:

- Is VMFS required?

- Which protocol should be used?

- Should vSphere storage integration be used?

To start making sensible design choices, the following information, at a minimum, is needed:

- Total/size of IOPS

- Capacity required

- Throughput

- Logical datastore design

- SLA

The requirement of VMFS is a key technical design choice and will limit the solution to iSCSI or FC-based hardware. In previous versions of vSphere, the advantages of VAAI could direct a designer toward VMFS, but with the launch of vSphere 5 VAAI, it is also supported for NAS devices.

From a VMware perspective, the platform is storage type agnostic. Other factors should be considered to form a pragmatic decision:

- Technical requirements of the workloads

- Project budget

- In-house expertise

- Existing vendor agreements

- Other functionality that can be offloaded or performed by the filer device (for example, deduplication with the SSD cache pool)

Examples of Recommended Best Practices

The following are examples of general storage best practices. In the real world, there are vendor-specific best practices and community-based implementations based on experience. The following examples illustrate the kinds of thought processes that are used in storage design and that may be expected in the VCAP5-DCD exam:

- Consider using dedicated physical networks for connectivity. If they are unavailable, consider the function of the traffic and logically separate it using network segmentation (for example, VLANs).

- Try to reduce latency by keeping the number of hops between the host and a storage device to a minimum.

- With network-based storage, evaluate enabling jumbo frames (which requires an MTU of 9,000). However, ensure that you are not moving or creating a bottleneck; configure the MTU size from end to end and across the board.

- Ensure that there are multiple NICs or paths to storage.

- Use two single-port connection interfaces (for example, HBA or NICs rather than dual or quad ports; ensure redundancy throughout the solution).

- Ensure driver-level redundancy by putting two different NICs from two separate vendors in a NIC teaming situation (for example, Broadcom and Intel on one vSwitch).

- Configure active–passive arrays to use the most recently used (MRU) load-balancing algorithm, and for active–active arrays use a fixed or round-robin algorithm. (See VMware KB 1011340 for more info.)

Network Design: Logical and Physical Design to Allow Applications to Flow

A VMware designer has two main concerns with network design:

- **The VMware platform**—This involves functionality and the SLA of the vSphere system.

- **The workload platform**—It's important to ensure that workloads have the network they require. (Confirm the infrastructure qualities.)

For the network component of vSphere design, the following information is required from the project discovery phases:

- Capacity of services required

- Number of physical NICs

- Number of vSwitches

When designing a network for a virtual platform, there is a very important aspect to consider. Is the design required to integrate with an existing physical network (that is, a brownfield site), or are you creating one from the ground up (that is, a greenfield site)?

In either case, you will more often than not be highly constrained with regard to design choices in this component layer. It is common for most networks of any notable size to have a dedicated network engineer or networking team with their own policies, best practices, and ideas. Thus, your role as a designer/architect is to ensure that the vSphere network meets the requirements for workloads on the platform and communicating/interacting with the physical world.

A brownfield site will most likely have existing policies, demarcation points, and logical segmentation. Your role here is to integrate by making the physical and virtual networks as transparent to the virtual workloads as possible. For example, load balancing algorithm settings must be compatible with physical networks, VLAN settings must be compatible within port groups, and MTU settings throughout the design must match with the physical network.

Within a greenfield site, you may be able to introduce items such as vApp networks with segmentation provided by logical virtual firewalls such as the vShield family. The advantage here could be to create DRS rules to ensure that vApp traffic never actually leaves the physical hosts and has little impact on the physical network interfaces or switches. This could have design impacts with regard to the complexity of the network design and costs of the networks (for example, lower number of links, bandwidth on the physical network required).

Although when implemented correctly a vApp network design is a valid and secure method of network management, many enterprises and security/risk professionals may not initially feel comfortable implementing web-facing and non-web-facing traffic on the same hosts, in the same networks, and so on. This is an example of a potential challenge from non-VMware professionals who may be misinformed or unfamiliar with the technology. A VMware architect will therefore be required to clarify and justify the decisions.

vNetworks: Planning from the Basics

As shown in Figure 4-6, the basic components of a vNetwork are guest NICs (vNICs), some type of virtual switch for connecting VMs to each other (vSphere Standard Switch [VSS] or vSphere Distributed Switch [VDS]), and links to the wider network made via physical NICs (pNICs)/uplinks.

- A guest VM is assigned to a port on a vSwitch. (Consider port binding type and the number of ports on a vSwitch.)
- The vSwitch has required networks defined using one or more port groups.
- The vSwitch configuration has a direct mapping with a physical switch via the host physical NIC and integrates with physical switch configuration (for example, port group settings need to match VLAN settings).

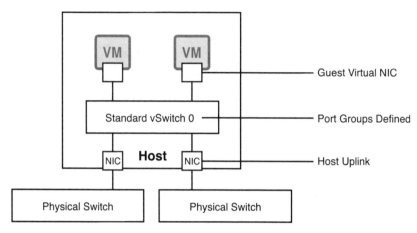

Figure 4-6 Basic Components of a Virtual Network

These are the basic rules for vSphere networking:

- An ESXi physical NIC can be assigned to only one vSwitch at a time. (For example, a host with five NICs can have a maximum of five vSwitches that can link to the outside world.)

- A vSwitch cannot connect directly to another vSwitch.

- Use the minimum number of vSwitches possible to meet the design requirements and after considering the infrastructure qualities.

Whether designing for a greenfield or brownfield network, there are a variety of key choices (shown in Figure 4-7) that a VMware platform designer needs to make or at least consider when planning the network layer.

It is uncommon to allow all devices in an enterprise to be able to communicate with each other without exception, control, or understanding of activity.

If it is unplanned or poorly planned, a flat network can run out of IP addresses within the range and require reconfiguration with different subnetting, potentially causing an outage or application issues. However, using a flat network can allow connections between every device on the network. This presents a couple of risks:

- Unauthorized access and privacy issues, such as seeing unencrypted data across the same network not being allowed from a security perspective

- Latency issues, such as a very chatty application or function using all the bandwidth you have in your connection media and affecting lots of applications

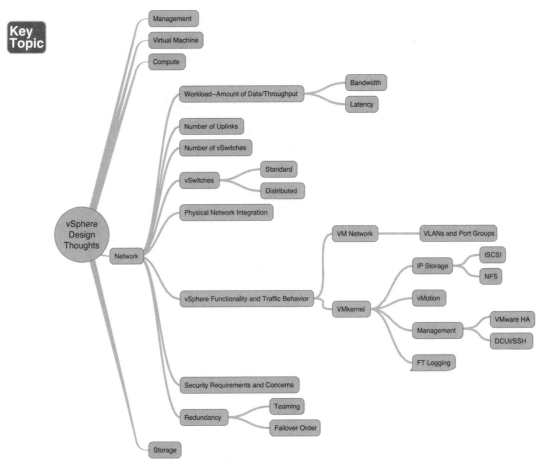

Figure 4-7   Network Design Considerations

Due to issues like these (and there are many more), it is very common to segment platforms into different networks based on a couple options:

- **Functionality or type (for example, traffic type)**—iSCSI storage is some-times separated from other traffic to prevent latency issues. (Or you can poten-tially use vSphere technology such as NOIC to mitigate risk.)

- **Security**—You may need to prevent access from other machines in the enterprise.

From a VMware perspective, there are a couple of types of networks:

- VMkernel connection traffic types:

    - IP storage (iSCSI and NFS v3)

    - Management/HA

    - vMotion

    - Fault tolerance (FT) logging

- Guest VM networks (for example, a production web server network that may be in a separate network from a production database that contains credit card data)

From a design point of view, it would be ideal to separate all these types of traffic to dedicated interfaces, both from the virtual world to the physical world. This is a best-case recommendation, but once you factor in hardware fault tolerance and bandwidth requirements for the traffic types, it could be unviable (that is, unsupportable from a cost or vendor standpoint) and, in many cases, not specifically needed. It could even be seen as overkill for the project use case. (For example, dedicating two 1 GB NICs to management in a chassis server with six 1 GB NICs with a utilization of less than 2% could be seen as bad design.)

It is common to logically separate or combine the VMkernel connection traffic types in different combinations, but understanding the impact is important. You need to note the function of each traffic type. What would happen if the operations depending on a particular connection suffered latency? Are there any security issues that should be understood? Once a decision has been made on what needs to be separated, how will the traffic be segmented? VMware enables you to use physical networks or logical separation by means of VLANs:

- **Virtual switch tagging (VST)**—VST is an accepted best practice whereby VLANs are applied at the vSwitch layer and integrated to the physical layer with the tags applied.

- **External switch tagging (EST)**—This method requires no vSphere configuration as the physical switch segments the traffic by adding VLAN information.

- **Virtual guest tagging (VGT)**—Segmentation (VLAN tags) are applied at the guest VM level.

How Should the Virtual Switch Layer Be Configured?

There are two basic types of vSwitch: standard and distributed. It is possible to decide which type of switch to use by considering the following:

- Functionality required

- Cost

- Ease of management

- Experience of vAdmins

Distributed vSwitches (VDS) are part of the vSphere Enterprise Plus edition.

With a large number of ESXi hosts and the use of standard vSwitches—even when functionality provided by distributed switches isn't being used—the level of management provided by VDS can be a benefit. Consider a service provider. Whenever a client requires another VLAN, an admin has to configure and update the port group settings correctly on every single ESXi host on every relevant vSwitch. Even if the functionality is possible with standard vSwitches, the use case of distributed switches could be justified to ensure quality and reduce the need for excessive operational processes.

How Many Physical NICs Do You Need?

You can determine how many physical NICs to use by considering the following:

- The amount of bandwidth required

- vSwitch configuration, including the number of switches and the logical segmentation technique

- The cost of the chassis and the number of slots

- Security requirements

- Hardware fault tolerance (so you create no single point of failure)

Creating a Logical Design

In various real-life projects, I have seen engineers constrained with regard to host choice. The enterprise may have one or two hardware providers with standardized specifications (for example, small—1U, 2 NICs, 1 physical CPU; medium—2U, 4 NICs, 2 physical CPUs; and large—4U, 4 NICs, and 4 physical CPUs). It is important to understand that ESXi hosts are not just machines hosting a single workload each; they are the core component of the vSphere platform and should be treated as a unique specification.

I have seen many engineers skip planning for host network design and just install ESXi on a machine of choice, log in to the box via the vSphere client, and then say, "How many physical NICs do we have?" "Aha, six pNICs! So that's two for VMware (management, vMotion), two for storage, and two for the VM networks." Although technically this configuration might work initially, the number of possible issues that could occur once workloads are placed or developed/scaled out on the platform is quite high. Think about the following:

- What happens when a hardware issue occurs? Is there enough bandwidth when a physical NIC fails?

- If a vMotion is initiated by DRS when a cluster is imbalanced, would this cause a HA event due to possible network latency?

- Are all guest workload owners happy, from a security perspective, to have logically separated networks and test, development, and production platform traffic on the same physical hosts or interfaces?

When presented with the need to integrate vNetwork into a design, how would you take the vNetwork basics/design thoughts and turn them into a suitable logical design? A network design process should include the following steps:

1. Identify the workloads the vNetwork has to support.

2. Identify the VMware functionality required (for example, vMotion, network storage, fault tolerance).

3. Consider the infrastructure qualities and other project factors (for example, cost, training).

4. Draw a high-level logical diagram and develop the design based on requirements and consider impacts.

5. Consult with other network teams to ensure suitability of the design (if teams exist).

6. Produce and agree on a logical network design with the project team.

For example, say that a software development company has a new virtualization strategy. The main purpose is to cut costs by consolidating five fully populated physical racks with an aging, nearly out-of-support physical hardware into two racks running vSphere and allow this infrastructure to support the growing business over the next three years.

From the information gathering stage, the following information was investigated:

- Workload and platform requirements for throughput and bandwidth

- How the platform was connected (for example, 1 GB or 10 GB, core and edge switches, associated multisite links, existing policies)

- What traffic types exist (for example, storage, guest workload networks), whether they need to be separated, and any specific operational requirements (for example, management must be on different physical interfaces than production workloads)

- Specific technology requirements (for example, vMotion and HA is required, but fault tolerance is not).

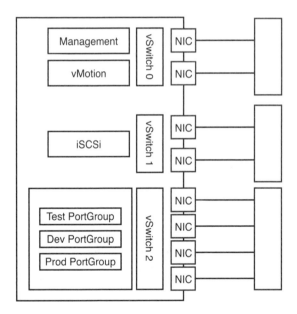

Figure 4-8   An Example of a Logical Diagram of a Virtual Network

Based on the information from the project life cycle, the logical diagram shown in Figure 4-8 was created. Note the following in this design example:

- VMware platform management traffic has been separated into network storage and virtual workloads.

- The storage network is separated physically due to a security requirement.

- Workloads are logically separated with port groups using 802.1q-specified VLANs. Four NICs are specified to ensure enough uplinks.

When this design was presented to the project team, there was a fear that over time the number of projects would increase, and testing/development platforms could impact production if a physical NIC failed.

This concern could be mitigated in various ways. First, it would be possible to use VMware's Network I/O Control. However, this would require distributed vSwitches rather than standard vSwitches. This could mean potentially incurring additional costs on vSphere licensing, needing more experienced VMware admins, and so on.

To support Network I/O Control as an option, additional logical designs should be created, showing the user-created network resource pools and ensuring that the production network port group is allocating sufficient resources (specified from metrics identified at the information gathering stage) during contention.

One point to highlight in this design is that VMware FT could potentially never realistically be used in production. VMware FT requires an additional VMkernel port marked for fault tolerance logging. The use of this additional traffic type on vSwitch0 could impact HA and DRS. Thus, adding this functionality may require additional network cards or additional port density on the underlying physical platform (for example, on top of rack switches), which would affect total cost, and this might be seen as totally unviable for the workload use case that VMware FT would protect.

Moving from the Logical Design to the Physical Design

Once a logical network has been designed and agreed on, it is time to analyze possible solutions and discuss with network professionals the specific network configurations and what hardware models vendors would recommend. Having an agreed-on logical design will help you make an informed decision on some or all of the following:

- The vendor make and model of the host NIC

- The number of NICs per card

- The physical switch types and vendor model

- Switch configuration info

Here are some guiding network design thoughts to consider:

- Separate networks based on VMware technology and the possible impact. For example, plan not to have iSCSI storage traffic and vMotion traffic sharing the same network and connections due to the possible impact on applications.

- Separate networks physically, where possible, or use a logical separation approach.

- Ensure that the solution is physically fault tolerant. Have no single points of failure (for example, use NIC teaming or multiple virtual VMkernel ports for management and HA).

- If using NIC teaming, confirm that, in the event of a NIC failure, the bandwidth meets workload requirements; otherwise, what's the point?

- Avoid STP (see VMware KB 1003804).

- If jumbo frames are configured, ensure that the correct MTU size is used throughout the network from end to end.

- Configure Cisco Discovery Protocol for troubleshooting using other tools and teams.

Compute and Host Design

An ESXi host is home to your virtual workload memory and CPU requests (Compute Capacity). It is your role as a vSphere designer/architect to create a platform that can adequately support all workloads to the required SLA and provide fault tolerance and a design that is as simple as possible for ease of deployment and maintenance.

An ESXi host can be seen as a building block (of memory and CPU resources – Compute layer) that can be scaled outward into a number of blocks as a cluster to allow fluctuations of workload demand to be met by migrating guest VMs across them in a dynamic fashion (for example, DRS using vMotion). An important part of vSphere platform design is to:

- Ensure that a building block is the correct size (see Figure 4-9:

- Provides correct CPU and memory functionality

- Can support maximum per-guest-VM maximums

- Is consistently configured

- Is supportable by the vendors (the physical host as well as VMware platform)

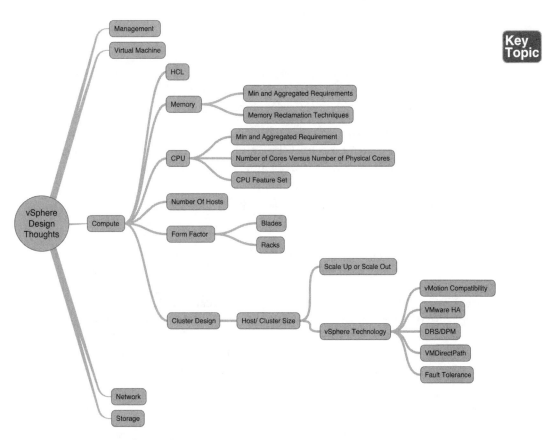

Figure 4-9 Compute Design Thoughts

How to Determine the Host Size and Number

There are various factors to consider when determining the size and number of hosts. First, each host must be able to run at least the maximum size of its expected virtual workload within the project scope. This information will come from the information gathering phase. At this stage, it is also worth considering the following:

- Aggregated CPU (MHz) and memory requirements (GB)

- The number of virtual CPUs to be hosted and the number of physical cores available

- Maximum utilization (for example, if the project SLA specifies to ensure that utilization never exceeds 75%, leave room for maintenance, overhead, and so on)

- Socket and core availability

- Future growth

Once the minimum host size has been identified, and the total amount of compute resources has been determined from the information gathering phase, what are the options for establishing the number of hosts to be used?

From the minimum workload size, it is possible to purchase a lower number of the biggest high-populated hosts (scale up) or obtain a higher number of smaller hosts (scale out). Table 4-3 shows some potential impacts of both approaches.

Table 4-3 Potential Impacts of Scale-up Versus Scale-out Approaches

Scale Up	Scale Out
Larger number of VMs possible per host	Smaller number of VMs per host (must consider max size of project workload and factor in future growth)
Growth for larger guest VM size in later platform life cycle or subsequent vSphere versions	Larger admin overhead; may require increased licensing for processes (for example, distributed switches, host profiles)
Larger impact to business if there is a host failure (for example, more workloads impacted, more VMs to restart under VMware HA)	Smaller number of VMs to restart under HA; if there is a low consolidation ratio per host, danger of fragmented resources in HA events
Longer times to take servers in and out of maintenance mode	
Large amount of capacity possibly wasted in VMware HA, depending on the admission control policy configured	

The following are some of the guiding best practices:

- Ensure that all host components are on the VMware Hardware Compatibility List.

- Ensure that all nodes in a cluster are compatible with vMotion. Use the CPU ID utility to ensure that existing hosts are compatible with newer purchases. Investigate the use of enhanced vMotion compatibility.

- Consider running, load testing, or "bedding in" each new host for 24 hours to ensure that components are tested before placing critical workloads on the platform.

- When configuring BIOS settings, enable hyperthreading and turn off all host CPU management features, such as SpeedStep. Give the hypervisor full control of compute resources.

- Design for initial project requirements and add for growth and other overheads.

- Ensure that all components are redundant and ensure that there are no single points of failure; when you consolidate workloads into a smaller number of physical devices, the impact of a failed component could be greater.

- Consider memory sharing gains from functions such as TPS; however, ensure that you understand the workload behaviors (for example, large page sizes do not deduplicate well until hosts hit levels of very high utilization, which may not be practical in the design).

- Observe configuration maximums (for example, 512 VMs per host, maximum number of logical CPUs).

- Leave extra capacity for items such as maintenance mode, upgrades, patching, and short-term surges in demand.

- Consider the VMware recommendation of around four to six vCPUs allocated per physical core.

- Configure hosts in a cluster in an identical manner (for example, slot settings, cable configurations, port numbers, and naming conventions). This will aid in troubleshooting, documentation, implementation with scripting and so on.

Management/Platform Design

Many vSphere admins see vCenter simply as a way into the environment. This is partly true from the perspective that virtual workloads will continue to operate in the event of a vCenter outage (for example, if there is no dependency). It is, however, a key component of the vSphere platform. In the event of a vCenter application outage, the following functions, among others, are affected:

- vMotion is not possible.

- DRS, Storage DRS, and DPM functionality are lost.

- Configuration changes to distributed switches and HA are not possible.

- Auto Deploy is unavailable (for example, new hosts cannot be introduced to the scheme).

The vCenter is also the central management server for all aspects of the virtual environment, from KVM functions at the guest virtual machine level to automated patching of ESXi hosts (with VMware Update Manager).

As shown in Figure 4-10, there are several key design choices for vSphere management.

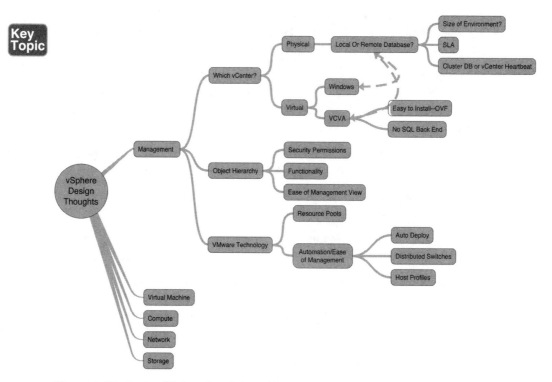

Figure 4-10 Design Choices for vSphere Management

As in previous sections of this chapter, I do not list all aspects of vCenter design here. Rather, I illustrate the design thoughts and how to relate the functionality to create a suitable design for a project or question in the VCAP5-DCD exam.

When faced with designing the vCenter platform, consider the following:

- Which vCenter type: physical or virtual? (See Table 4-4 for design choice impacts in this case.)

- If virtual, which version?

- Whether to use a remote or local database

- vCenter sizing and impact (server and database)

- Use a management cluster?

- Is Linked Mode required?

Table 4-4   Design Choice Impacts for Virtual and Physical vCenter Deployments

Physical Deployments	Virtual Deployments
Required for internal policy/regulatory compliance?	Competition with other guests for resources
Not impacted by a VMware host outage	Affected by VMware outage if hosted on same platform it is managing
Dedicated resources from physical machine	Take advantage of virtualization benefits (for example, portability, backup, hardware abstraction)
Extra cost to protect for outage (VMware vCenter Heartbeat)	Can be protected with VMware HA
Bound to hardware (server life cycle may be limited)	Transparently migrated to new hardware

There are two main types of deployment destination for the vCenter: physical deployment to hardware on a Windows machine or a virtual machine version. Both destinations have advantages and disadvantages. One important design question that could guide toward a physical or virtual deployment is "How long can the company tolerate a vCenter outage?" While the vCenter is a critical server role, the guest virtual machines will continue to function during a vCenter outage. If the business can withstand the loss of these types of functionality until vCenter connectivity is restored, a single virtual vCenter protected by VMware HA would be perfectly adequate.

After deciding on virtual or physical, you need to choose one of the two types of virtual vCenter Server:

- Windows based

- The Linux appliance–based vCenter Server Appliance (VCSA)

What factors should be considered in making the choice? The VCSA is a Linux-based operating system with a prebuilt installation of vCenter Server. It is extremely easy to configure via an OVF import and unique configuration that offers prompts and is mainly web driven (for example, database connection, password/IP addressing).

There is no difference between the two types of servers from an access or use perspective, however:

- SQL is not an option for the underlying VCSA database.

- Items that are dependent on Windows technology are not possible with the VCSA (for example, linked clones with VMware View, vCenter Linked Mode).

- The virtual appliance is intended for small deployments (for example, roughly 5 hosts and 50 VMs with the embedded DB2 database).

The VCSA, which is licensed with vSphere and uses a Linux OS, does not need extra licensing for Windows or, in the case of embedded databases, a license for a production-level database.

You can take care of factors such as DR by backing up the VCSA or underlying database regularly and simply redeploying in the event of a failure.

If the items that are currently unsupported are not platform requirements, the advantages of functionality such as SSO, Auto Deploy, Syslog Collector, and ESXi Dump Collector being made available by a single check box selection and not requiring a lengthy installation process make the VCSA use case very compelling.

For full functionality in the VMware product range, extendibility, and integration with existing backup processes, the Windows version checks a lot of the boxes. A nice rule of thumb for a VMware designer/architect is to keep it simple. In most modern enterprises, there will be a form of production database, normally supported by a dedicated database administrator. Here, a VMware designer could use the scripts from the vCenter Server CD or installation ISO, which can be used to produce a nice implementation and a high-level technical guide for a competent DBA on how to create, populate, and run the vCenter Server database on SQL and Oracle.

By utilizing in-house expertise with existing database technology and providing technical information required to support it, you can manage the vCenter database like any other important database. All that is required is to install vCenter Server on the destination virtual machine and link the installation to the database. If a database solution suitable for hosting the vCenter Server database is not available for some reason, it is possible to create a standalone one that is local to the vCenter Server. This is the default for simple installations, and it creates a local SQL-based database. This is suitable for small installations similar to the VCSA embedded database deployment. There are operational issues, such as backup and recovery model configuration. (Be careful of transaction logs size, or, in the case of simple recovery, the RPO needed for the system.)

One consideration that must be addressed both for hosting the vCenter Server remotely using an existing production database and installing locally is an understanding of how big the vCenter is now and how big it will be over a set period of time (normally determined by the project requirements—for example, 3 years) both from a server specification requirement (for example, memory and CPU requirements) and database (size in GB).

These considerations depend on items such as the number of VMs and hosts running in the environment and also the number of other objects, such as resource pools. There are two quick ways to estimate this: using the What If Calculator from the vSphere client or by using the vCenter sizing Excel spreadsheet for Microsoft SQL and Oracle.

A couple of final points to consider with regard to vCenter Server design are the use of a management cluster and Linked Mode. With strategies such as "virtualize first" appearing in enterprises, it is common for the virtual platforms to host systems such as DNS, DHCP, and Active Directory, and so on. These services are critical to the enterprise but are not workloads that application-driven projects would reveal in any great detail. It may be perfectly viable to run these systems within the same platform as the user applications they serve. What happens if the hosts fail or there is some dependency?

In the case of DNS and AD, applications will need to start in the correct order (for example, after DNS and AD, to be able to resolve the name of the AD domain and then authenticate to it). Setting startup priorities with VMware HA can help you avoid issues in the event of a failure. The vCenter may depend on such technologies, and, since there is a significant impact if it fails, it should be considered in this manner (for example, DNS, AD, database, then vCenter). Instead of hosting these management services within the same platform as the user workloads, you could have the enterprise build a dedicated smaller management cluster that is designed to ensure service and availability of these services for the workloads. There are obviously increased hardware and licensing factors to consider; however, the services are not susceptible to impact from application workloads monopolizing host resources. Functionality such as Auto Deploy allows full functionality if all hosts supporting the workloads are powered off while the management cluster (providing Auto Deploy) is left powered on. If both the vCenter Server and Auto Deploy server exist on the same platform as the ESXi servers, a full host outage would result in the entire system being down due to no ESXi images being deliverable.

A final consideration for the design of vCenter Server is the use of Linked Mode. This functionality allows a VM admin to log in to view multiple vCenter platforms at the same time by logging into just one. For example, say that a large enterprise has two datacenters: a production site and a DR site. It could be possible to have a dedicated vSphere platform and vCenter installation at either site. There may be a requirement for vAdmins to log in to a system and see both datacenters for monitoring and configuration. Both sites and databases would have their own databases and vCenter installations, independent of each other, for backup and DR purposes.

Another use case would be using Linked Mode when a system has been scaled past the number of powered-on VMs or other configuration maximums. By combining vCenter Servers in a single pane of glass, VM admins can manage a large estate in a clearer manner. Items such as object searching would span the whole platform.

The Importance of vMotion, VMware HA, and Fault Tolerance

VMware infrastructure touches every part of the datacenter; for many people (including me), this is the most interesting and exciting reason to work and study it. However, the basic concept is that you are essentially taking workloads of varied criticality that are happily running (or can be) on physical hardware and placing them together with other workloads on shared infrastructure. When things are running well, it's great. In the event of contention, maintenance requirements, or component failures, understanding the impact is vital to providing a good platform for your client.

Physical hardware is a safe place for workloads. It can be seen as simple and low risk for deployment. Modern server platforms have lots of CPUs and redundant parts such as power supplies, fans, and so on. Also, there is a nice big air gap between systems that have different security profiles.

From a high level, deploying workloads in a virtual infrastructure can be seen as a more risky approach than using physical hardware. You are taking all those happy redundant servers and placing them on a shared infrastructure. The workloads may now have to compete for resources, have fewer redundant parts per physical host, and have logical separation rather than an air gap.

"I'm not sure if I like to put all my eggs in one basket—especially the important eggs!" I've heard this kind of statement from various businesses and IT professionals during design discussions, defenses, and walkthroughs.

Enter vMotion, VMware HA, and FT. These VMware functions not only mitigate concerns but can add more value and flexibility. When configured correctly, VMware infrastructure can provide a more reliable and arguably equally secure platform for workloads of all criticality levels.

Admission Control, and I Don't Have the Power, Captain!

VMware HA can, in some sense, be configured in a few clicks, and the admin can just walk away. However, will it work as expected? Consider its function: "To restart machines on a working host when another host in the cluster has failed." VMware HA is fantastic technology from this perspective; its primary function is to restart VMs when a hardware failure has occurred. How does a designer consider this? Through a DR plan! (This is covered in more detail in Chapter 6, "Project Execution").

VMware HA could be considered a replacement for running around the datacenter when a rack or multiple racks have power issues. The engineer knows which machines to start up first, and in what order, for applications. If the engineer just restarted them in a random order, then the application tiers or dependencies might not start up correctly, and the systems might not return. Basically, DR and failure states need planning; therefore, VMware HA restart processes and capabilities need planning, too.

Two key HA design considerations are restart capability and restart order. When HA is configured, the function reserves a specific amount of resources for a disaster. This is the amount of resources it calculates it will need to restart VMs when a host or multiple hosts fail.

How do you understand and predict the resources required for VMware HA to meet your specific project requirements? The answer: by configuring admission control policies.

An admission control policy is a setting that tells VMware HA how to calculate the amount of resources it needs to reserve for a cluster. It uses a combination of memory and CPU reservation configuration or a default low reservation if no configuration exists. (It is wise to ensure that this does not affect the platform design.)

There are four choices with admission control policy:

- Host Failure Hosts Tolerate

- Percentage of CPU and Memory

- Dedicated Failover Host(s)

- Violate Failover Restraints

NOTE Refer to the *VMware vSphere 5 Availability Guide* (pages 18–22) for worked examples of calculations for admission control based on project requirements.

Restart Priority

What happens when a rack loses power or an integration service in a multitier application fails? Even if the systems are restarted, an incorrect order could render the application nonfunctional, even if the guest VMs are running. By taking information from the entity dependency diagrams and mapping out the restart order, VMware HA can be configured with either cluster-wide or specific guest virtual machine restart orders, based on priorities. Unfortunately, vApp power-down or startup orders are not respected, and even with this configuration, VMware HA Startup order cannot be guaranteed at the OS or application service level (because VMs are just powered on, VMware HA does not wait for application services to start). In the real world, an analyst or engineer may need to inspect the application status at the time of a VMware HA event.

Personally, I treat a VMware HA event as a function that will restart as many of the user workloads as possible, and, from testing the workloads, create a document that shows application operational tasks for applications that are not gracefully restarted in a VMware HA event.

VMware HA is very simple to configure. It's so easy, in fact, that an engineer could configure an option and leave it running until the dreaded moment when a failure occurs and the behavior is not as expected. A properly planned DR consideration is normally required for all projects; if not defined explicitly, the infrastructure qualities guide the designer to consider the expectations for the workloads and the ability to recover.

Although VMware HA is simple to configure, the process and impacts of configuration in various scenarios can be quite complex. Once you're armed with the design questions and thought processes from this chapter, I highly recommend that you read the excellent *VMware vSphere 5 Clustering Technical Deepdive* by Frank Denneman and Duncan Epping before you complete a full real-life design and attempt the VCAP5-DCD exam.

Here are some guiding best practices to consider when enabling VMware HA and DRS:

- If ESXi is used with lockdown mode enabled, ensure that it is possible to access the DCUI of each host in the cluster (for example, DRAC, ILO). Without this access, lockdown mode cannot be disabled. (If the vCenter is offline) an engineer will not be able to log directly in to the ESXi host running the vCenter to fix issues.

- If DRS is in fully automated mode and host-to-vCenter communication is not functional, no guest migrations will occur. If the cluster becomes imbalanced, business application performance may be affected. Thus, you should ensure that resource requirements for critical applications are satisfied (for example, using reservations or ensuring adequate cluster size).

- Disable a virtual vCenter guest machine from automated DRS migrations. This ensures that the engineer will know exactly which host to log in to directly, without wasting precious time searching for the vCenter. (A DRS rule could be used for this consideration.)

- As VMware HA functionality continues in the event of a vCenter outage, a virtual vCenter can be protected just like any other guest machine. However, consider the restart priority of the vCenter guest virtual machine, and also consider the slot size if a reservation has been used.

Guest Machine Placement

With fully automated DRS, and because within clusters it is recommended to configure all hosts in the same manner throughout, some might think that guest virtual machine placement is irrelevant. The opposite is true: Virtual machine placement can have a dramatic impact on the infrastructure qualities.

For example, consider several guest virtual machines that have similar roles. These guests were all made from the same initial template, are running the same operating system, and are performing similar activities, such as web hosting logically underneath a load balancer. The memory usage for these VMs will be very similar. By understanding the function of these boxes, an administrator can place these machines on the same host.

The TPS process by default runs every 60 minutes, and it gradually takes the memory pages in 4 K chunks and deduplicates the data. By ensuring that similar guest virtual machines are on the same host, you can maximize memory consolidation.

In the real world, the placement of VMs within a cluster can be easily controlled with a DRS rule to ensure that 50% of web servers are placed on one host and another 50% of web servers are placed on another host. This would maximize memory consolidation using TPS; however, it would also take into consideration platform availability. A design drawback here could be the restart time if a VMware HA event takes place.

Now What Do I Do?

The VCP exam tests specific knowledge of functions, such as what is VMware HA, and what is DRS? The VCAP5-DCD exam is aimed at understanding why and how you should be configuring a solution to meet a certain requirement.

This book has been created to help you understand how to study and pass the exam. It is impossible to discuss all the possible variations and requirements. The virtualization arena is expanding and evolving every day. I recommend that you read about the subject and keep up to date on current and emerging technologies.

Before you take the exam, complete the tasks in the following section to develop a process to create and transition between logical and physical designs. Practice creating and reviewing diagrams from case studies. (The VMware website has several.) Read around the blueprint subjects and consider the technical merits. Read up on the accepted best practices and understand advantages and disadvantages of the technologies and the use cases.

The VCAP5-DCD exam may not specifically ask for technical details, but you must show an understanding of when to use a particular VMware technology and how to represent it when applied to a particular scenario. Your role if you are a platform or VMware architect is varied, but one core skill is the ability to take a technology you have never used, apply a process to research its merits, and apply use cases to a business problem to determine whether the business should use that technology. At this point, creating a logical design and transitioning to a physical design can be completed with the help of vendors or subject matter experts.

Exam Preparation Tasks

Review All Key Topics

Review the most important topics in the chapter, noted with the key topics icon in the outer margin of the page. Table 4-5 lists these key topics and the page number on which each is found.

Table 4-5 Key Topics

Key Topic Element	Description	Page
Paragraph	The vSphere platform components	60
Figure 4-5	Design choices for the storage component of vSphere platforms	69
Figure 4-7	Network design thoughts	76
Figure 4-9	Compute design thoughts	83
Figure 4-10	Design choices for vSphere management	86

Design Scenario

You are a vSphere architect at a large enterprise. The business has just purchased a rival company and has requested a virtual platform to replace the aging physical-based platform. The existing workloads will be dealt with as part of another project.

The immediate requirement is to host two standard platform applications:

- Microsoft Exchange
- Microsoft SharePoint

Here is a summary of requirements from the high-level business brief:

- The number of users for this system initially is 12,000.
- RTO is 4 business hours, and RPO is 12 business hours.
- DR will be provided by SAN-based snapshots and offsite LTO5 tapes.
- Vendor support must be maintained.

Design a suitable platform for this scenario. Note the process you used to complete this task to create a checklist for future design work and as an approach in the final exam.

These are the types of deliverables you should aim to create for each vSphere component layer:

- Conceptual design
- Logical design
- A physical design using vendor best practices and recommendations

Once you have created a design, consider the infrastructure qualities and annotate the diagrams with components that may be improved, and possible impacts. Confirm that the design meets the requirements.

Definitions of Key Terms

Define the following key terms from this chapter and check your answers in the glossary.

Physical design, Compute layer, Network throughput, Storage IOPS

Review Questions

The answers to these review questions are in Appendix A.

1. According to HA best practices, which of the following admission control policies is most appropriate for a cluster of hosts with virtual machines of very different memory and CPU reservations?

    a. CPU and Memory % Configuration

    b. Number of Hosts Tolerate

    c. Failover Host

2. A requirement in a server consolidation project states: "The consolidation ratio must be as high as possible." This has resulted in a lower number of larger-capacity hosts in the vSphere HA cluster. Which of the following is true?

    a. The restart time of a VM could be greater than when using smaller hosts.

    b. The restart time of a VM could be lower than when using smaller hosts.

3. A host has three dual-port network cards. What is the maximum number of vSwitches that can be integrated with the physical network, assuming that network redundancy is not a requirement?

    a. 3

    b. 6

    c. 256

    d. 512

4. As a platform designer, you have been asked to create a design for a vSphere 5 platform. Based on existing capacity state analysis, the platform will require 30 hosts and 250 guest VMs. Due to an existing vendor relationship with the enterprise, the preferred database for all datacenter systems is Microsoft SQL 2008. Which of the following vCenter deployments can be used based on this constraint?

    a. VCSA with a remote Microsoft SQL 2008 database

    b. Windows-based vCenter with a local Microsoft SQL 2008 database

    c. VCSA with an embedded Microsoft database

    d. Any of the above would meet the requirements.

5. RTO and RPO requirements can have a direct impact on the size and number of virtual datastores used in a vSphere platform.

    a. True

    b. False

6. You are a platform designer constructing a physical design from an existing approved logical design. Out of the vendor proposals, there are two proposed solutions that could be used. Which of the following options is the most important factor when making a decision?

    a. Community and vendor-based best practices

    b. Existing vendor relationships

    c. Project requirements

    d. Project budget

This chapter covers the following subjects:

- **Virtual Machines—From the Design Perspective:** This section explains what to explore and consider when creating a guest virtual machine.

- **Guest Virtual Machine Component Considerations:** This section covers various rules of thumb for guest virtual machine design and management.

- **OVFs:** This section describes the importance and potential use cases of the open virtualization format.

This chapter covers the following objective of the VCAP-DCD5 blueprint: Objective 3.5, "Determine virtual machine configuration for a vSphere 5 physical design."

CHAPTER 5

Virtual Machine Design

Until this point in the book, we have considered designing and building the vSphere platform on which each guest VM runs. This is an important and interesting aspect for a vAdmin, but it definitely does not stop there. As a VMware engineer, you may not actually manage the guest operating systems. However, it is very important to remember that user applications run within guest operating systems. This is the environment where users' work is actually completed and their data is processed. Good virtual machine design can have a dramatic impact on application performance and other business or project objectives.

"Do I Know This Already?" Quiz

The "Do I Know This Already?" quiz allows you to assess whether you should read this entire chapter or simply jump to the "Exam Preparation Tasks" section for review. If you are in doubt, read the entire chapter. Table 5-1 outlines the major headings in this chapter and the corresponding "Do I Know This Already?" quiz questions. You can find the answers in Appendix A, "Answers to the 'Do I Know This Already?' and Chapter Review Questions."

Table 5-1   Do I Know This Already?" Foundation Topics Section-to-Question Mapping

Foundations Topics Section	Questions Covered in This Section
Virtual Machines—From the Design Perspective	3, 4
Guest Virtual Machine Component Considerations	1, 2, 5, 6, 9, 10–12, 14, 15
OVFs	7, 8, 13

1. A guest virtual machine has 4 GB of memory allocated to it. What is the size of the swap file?

   a. 4 GB minus the reservation

   b. The VM limit configuration minus the reservation

   c. Always 4 GB

2. An application is in its final stage of testing. There is a load test planned for 2 a.m. Which of the following would enable a suitable baseline to be derived, and, from a design perspective, not impact the platform?

   a. Configure a VM memory and CPU limit to ensure zero impact on other user applications

   b. Configure a memory and CPU reservation to guarantee a level of resources for load performance evaluation

   c. Amend share values to high

3. Which of the following does vApp functionality require?

   a. DRS enabled

   b. DRS enabled in fully automated mode

   c. A proposed vendor

4. A vApp can hold virtual machines and nested vApps.

   a. True

   b. False

5. A virtual machine template always has a swap file.

   a. True

   b. False

6. You have been asked to design a virtual machine for an as-yet-unwritten application. The high-level requirements are known, but aspects such as workload and application behavior (for example, memory driven, CPU driven) are not yet determined. Which of the following scaling approached would best suit this scenario?

   a. Predictive

   b. Adaptive

7. You are a member of a project team that consists of the following:

A business user (based in the UK)

Two software developers (based in the UK)

Two software testers (based in the United States and India)

One platform engineer (based in the UK)

The team requires multiple environments of the same infrastructure to work within the software development life cycle. Each environment consists of two web servers, a load balancer virtual appliance, an application server, and a database server. Which of the following would allow ease of management and deployment?

    a. Create a single virtual machine template and deploy servers as required for each stage of the SDLC (development, testing, staging, production).

    b. Create a single vApp that consists of the five servers. Use this as a deployment object for each stage of the SDLC.

    c. Create a single environment in vSphere 5 and allow users who are delegated rights to use snapshots and clones to allow the team to work between the stages.

8. Within the same scenario described in question 7, how would the server builds of each stage be easily shared and used between the teams in the United States and India without breaking guest operating system EULAs?

    a. Convert the template used for the builds to a VM. Export the VM as an OVF and present the file to the team.

    b. Export the vApp consisting of all server roles as an OVF.

    c. Create a single environment in vSphere 5 and allow users who are delegated rights to use snapshots and clones to allow the team to work between the stages.

9. You are a vSphere engineer working on a new vSphere 5 platform for an internal customer. Your platform consists of two sites. One site is a running production environment, and the other is a limited-capacity site for DR. The link between sites is 100 MB. Due to internal compliance requirements, the production systems are based on separate clusters to test systems. Fully automated DRS and DPM are to be used. Which of the following would minimize network bandwidth usage for replication of VMs and still allow vMotion functionality without impact to RTO or RPO?

   a. At the cluster level, configure the default swap file location to local storage.

   b. Configure traffic shaping to ensure that 30% of the network is used for replication.

   c. Configure vSphere network shares to prioritize network usage on the 100 MB line.

10. A platform consists of 20 applications and 230 guest VMs running on 20 hosts. Over a weekend, the operations team would like to perform maintenance on all hosts and some unpatched VMs. There are agreed outages during the weekend for each application. However, outside these times, the performance of the applications must meet normal requirements.

   The operations team has expertise in hardware and the patching processes but very little knowledge of the applications and server relationships. Which of the following would be the best course of action?

   a. Create a vApp for each application and configure the startup and shutdown order.

   b. Create a PowerShell script to control the startup and shutdown order.

   c. Specify restart priority in the VMware HA GUI.

11. vSphere HA does not recognize vApp startup order.

   a. True

   b. False

12. An application consists of five servers. The application requires specific IP addresses to be configured for listener servers. Which of the following configurations would satisfy the requirement?

   a. Configure a transient IP address pool and enter the range 192.168.117.23#5.

   b. Configure a transient IP address and enter the range 192.168.117.23-8.

13. An OVF can be configured with a EULA to be accepted before the servers are imported.

   a. True

   b. False

14. A custom application is created in-house; various services are required to be started in a specific order. It appears that the time it takes to start these services can vary, depending on a data feed from a third party. How should the vApp be configured with regard to startup order to enable effective management of the servers?

   a. Add a large wait time between servers on startup order to ensure that the data feed is responding.

   b. Because the feed is a variable and third-party solution, a vApp cannot be used to control the startup order of the application.

   c. Configure the vApp to wait for VMware tools to be ready on each server. At the guest operating system level, ensure that the VMware tools service is dependent on the custom application services.

15. You are a consultant called to investigate an HA failure. The platform consists of 6 hosts and 100 VMs. Of these 100 VMs, 80 are VDI machines used by a call center. Theoretically, the system is overcommitted in memory by 150%; however, under normal working conditions, the memory requirement is supported. The logs show that the HA task was successful; however, a large number of VDI machines failed to restart in sufficient time for the RTO. What could be the cause of the error?

   a. Shared memory is being used to increase the consolidation ratio. This uses TPS and requires the process to run several times to allow the VMs to run. Add more ESXi hosts or reduce the VM reservations.

   b. HA is reserving too much memory. Enable violation requirements.

   c. VM monitoring was disabled. Keep it enabled where possible.

Foundation Topics

Virtual Machines—From the Design Perspective

The concept of a virtual machine is covered in the prerequisite VCP5 certification; however, this chapter reviews the basics from a unique perspective in order to establish some design considerations and processes.

A virtual machine is the software equivalent of an actual physical machine. In the realm of the datacenter, an engineer normally has two considerations:

- Turning production physical machines into software (P2V)

- Deploying applications in a virtualized environment

One of the major advantages of virtualization is the ability to start with an existing working server estate and consolidate the workloads into fewer physical hosts. Logically the applications will be identical. Workloads may vary, but if done correctly, virtualization offers advantages such as savings in management, power, and costs.

People commonly ask me, "How much slower is a virtual machine than a physical machine?" The assumption that virtual machines are slower by default than physical machines is common. A key challenge for a VMware architect is to educate users to think about the application and the workloads running on them.

When a physical box is selected and built, it is common to have a piece of hardware that will never stress the system above 20% to 30% utilization when used at expected workloads. Such an approach leads to a substantial waste of resources, both in requirement and associated management costs, and also in terms of energy use and the consequent impact on the environment. Physical hardware capability has substantially overtaken the normal user application workload requirements.

The use of physical machines may hide a multitude of sins at a datacenter. In software development, it is possible to conceal poor application performance by throwing hardware at it to hide the bottlenecks or at least move them away from the current state of workload. In some cases a piece of hardware could be so overspecified that such problems would go unnoticed. While poor design is the cause of potential faults, hardware overspecification is a common real-life issue.

The vSphere admin who is responsible for setting up a VM will take an entire floor of server racks and place them nicely in a blade chassis, with all its redundancy and ease of management. If this setup is incorrectly researched or planned, a virtual version of the existing hardware estate may not live up to expectations. The admin may hear unwelcome remarks such as "It worked in physical" or "It doesn't work in a VM."

How does a vSphere admin tackle such a situation? You'll learn the answer in the next section.

It's All About the Application

Virtualizing an application is not the same as installing software on hardware. Although the operating system is normally unaware of the fact that it's being virtualized, it uses resources provided by the VMkernel. The main consideration is that the resources are not dedicated; rather, they are shared with other virtual machines.

The VMkernel has functionality that actively manages and attempts to avoid resource contention. Depending on the virtual workload behavior and other guest virtual machines running on the platform, however, contention can occur. By understanding how the virtual workload will behave, and by planning the configuration of the guest VMs, you can avoid user impact.

Where to Start: Guest VM Design Choices

As with a project initiation, the primary focus in virtualizing an application is the aim or vision. The virtual machine needs to provide a stable environment for the application in order to complete its role. You need to talk to the users and the software vendor or developers if the application is being developed in-house.

To design a virtual machine to deliver an application, a few questions and design thoughts should spring to mind (see Figure 5-1 for more guest virtual machine design choices):

- What does it do?

- Is it memory driven or CPU driven?

- What is the anticipated workload?

  - Number of users

  - Amount of data

  - Times of use, including peaks

- What is the expected growth over the period of usage (for example, 3 years)?

- What are the minimum requirements (for example, initially, in 1 year, over the life of contract)?

- What are the RTO and RPO requirements?

- What are the licensing and vendor support needs?

Key Topic

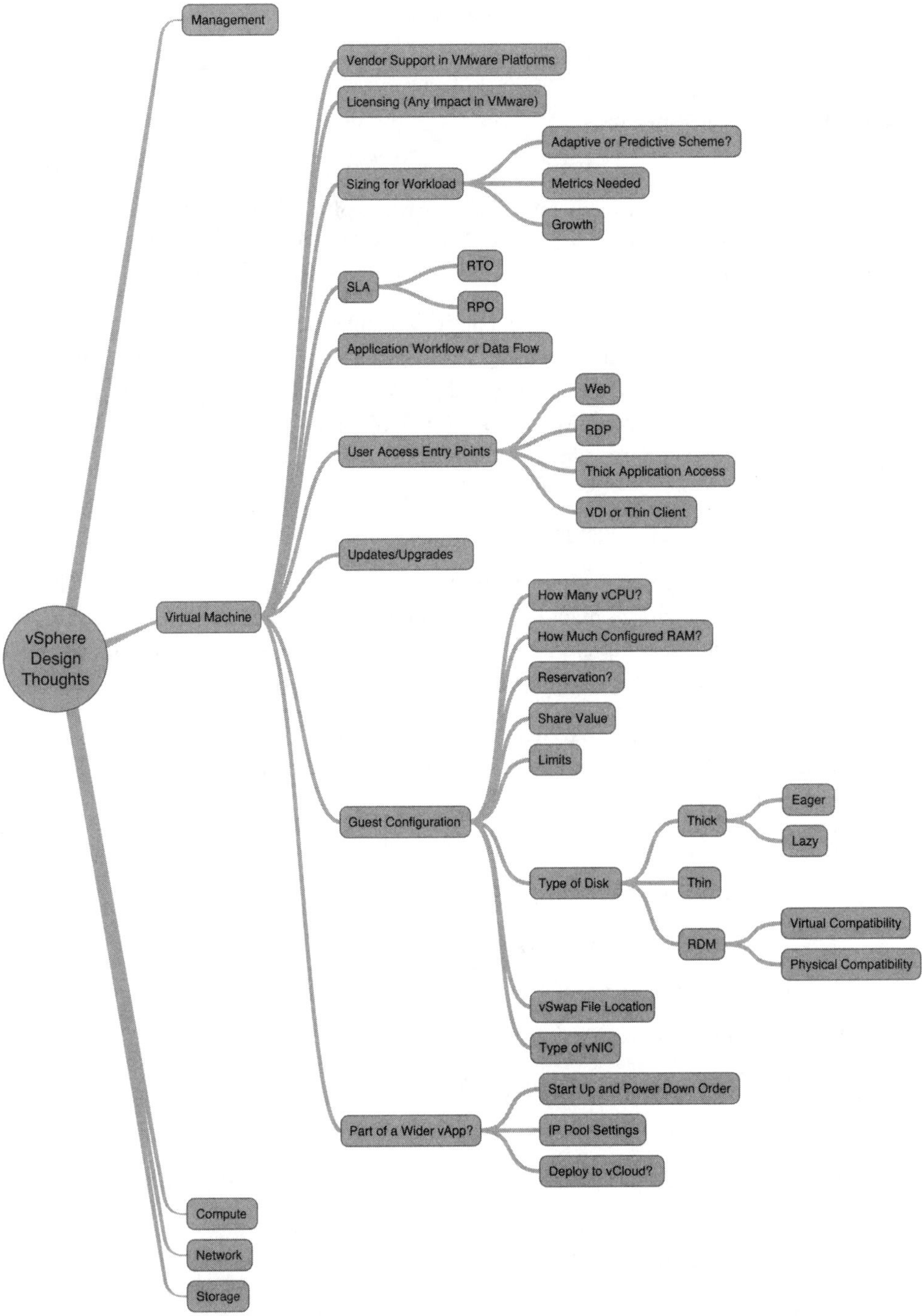

Figure 5-1 Guest Virtual Machine Design Choices

- What is the application work flow? Is the application dependent on other factors (that is, other application processes finishing successfully)?

- What are the entry points, and what is the mode of access (for example, web, thin client, RDP)?

- How frequently is the application updated, and what effects do those updates have on the software and applications?

Design Approaches

There are two types of scaling approaches in virtual platforms: adaptive *and* predictive. Both approaches are usable; however, a designer must work out which is the best approach for each project.

The *adaptive approach* to guest virtual machine design is a major advantage that virtualization technology brings to the datacenter. It allows a guest VM to be created initially on a few metrics or high-level requirements (a limited budget, for example) and scaled (that is, grown, not shrunk) through the virtual machine life cycle. In many cases, this scaling can be performed hot/live without outage/downtime to the running applications.

The *predictive approach*, on the other hand, requires more planning and research, and you must know the metrics before deployment. The advantage here is that once the VM has been deployed, only application maintenance is required. The application requirements are known, and the business understands how the requirements are going to be delivered.

In some instances, a combination of both approaches might be best. As a designer, you need to establish the minimum baseline for an application to perform under the required load and be successful—and to also have no impact on other applications. At the beginning of the life cycle, a business or developer may have limited experience with the application; there will be a learning period for both of them. By working together and understanding the key metrics, a stable platform should be possible—and this is the key to successful deployment.

The following are examples of metrics to consider:

- **CPU MHz used & CPU Ready values**—The amount of CPU used, whether the platform is fit for the purpose from the CPU's perspective; providing CPU time when requested.

- **Memory**—Consumed memory and shared memory. It's important to understand the possible savings and application performance with TPS and the impact for HA.

- **Ballooning**—Guest memory implications when the host is over-committed on memory. Does the application perform satisfactorily under contention?

- **Storage space, I/O requirements, and queue length**—Storage capacity, performance needs, and performance monitoring. What does the workload need to have from a storage perspective to adequately perform work (highly read/write or both)?

In real life, it is useful to consider the technical limitations with the adaptive scaling technique. VMware platforms are expected to be highly flexible and elastic when needed. The systems do have limits, however. For example, I've seen a limitation on a live application hosted in a vCloud datacenter-hosted provider platform. The multitier web application consumed 8 GB of memory at the web server, with 100 users. The system was declared production ready for the initial workload. The vCloud provider provided memory to the organization pool at a fixed cost per gigabyte per month. As the application acceptance grew, so did the memory requirements. Because the memory technically could be added hot (because it was allowed by the guest operating systems accepting the memory change), the company made the business decision to add memory only when required and save on running costs throughout the term of use. The first few times, this process worked correctly, and the process became business as usual. At one point, however, the business was unable to add the required memory without a power-off. This happened because of a limitation of hot-add memory being 16 times the power-on value (see VMware KB 2020846).

What Should a VM Contain?

You need to consider a variety of factors regarding what to install on a VM. Personally, I try to keep each machine as light as possible in all the resources and enable functionality when needed. A general rule of thumb is to configure a virtual machine as recommended by the vendor for the application it is going to run. For example, if an application recommends three logical drives, create them as recommended; however, from a virtual perspective, ensure that you consider the storage best practices (for example, type of disk [thin, thick, RDM], driver to be used for the virtual disk, mode for the disks) and ensure that each logical drive is a separate virtual disk file.

VMware recommends that its tools, including the following, be installed into every virtual machine running in the platform. What exactly are they?

VMware tools provide:

- Enhanced drivers (for example, graphics, mouse performance, virtual disk, NIC drivers)

- Time synchronization functionality

- Memory management drivers, such as a balloon driver

- Copy/paste functionality between VM and other machines via clients

- Quiescing functionality for crash-consistent snapshots

- Heartbeat mechanism used in VMware HA

- VMware Perfmon DLL functionality (with extra counters for VMware metrics)

- Scripting ability

As this list indicates, VMware tools are more than just graphics and NIC drivers. They are essential to a stable platform, and if used correctly, they can be used to automate various processes. When you upgrade to a new version of ESXi, you should upgrade the VMware tools as well to match the version.

The virtual machine hardware level is the collection of devices that are presented to the guest operating systems. As with physical machines, improvements or changes are made at each release. Upgrade Virtual Machine Hardware is a small and crucial function in the vSphere GUI, and many people forget about it. From a design perspective, however, it is an important consideration.

vSphere editions can support only certain hardware versions. For example, vSphere 4 cannot support hardware version 9. (The complete list is detailed in VMware KB 1003746.) In general, this might not cause worry; however, consider the following scenario: Say that a company is running various complex multitier applications on a vSphere 4.1 platform. The system consists of two clusters. Both clusters are running DRS in fully automated mode. Cluster A and B are identical in physical attributes; however, for day-to-day operations, cluster A is running production applications, and cluster B is a test/development cluster. In case of a disaster, cluster B is used for DR purposes. The RTO requirement is 15 minutes.

A vSphere 5 upgrade is scheduled for a transformation project, and cluster A is successfully upgraded. If the guest virtual machines are also upgraded to the latest hardware level, the virtual machines will not be able to run on the other cluster until it is upgraded as well, thus possibly violating the RTO requirement until the full upgrade occurs.

A more suitable upgrade process would be to upgrade all clusters that have dependencies in the design. The platform is, at that point, recoverable between clusters. Thus, upgrading the virtual machine hardware after this point would not affect the RTO.

For larger-scale upgrades, vSphere Update Manager can prevent such RTO violations by using a two-step orchestrated process which ensures that hosts are updated first, followed by the VMs.

In an upgrade scenario, you need to ensure that the process is followed in the correct order and complete the platform upgrade with a planned approach. It is important to understand the impact of each stage of the upgrade process.

Similarly to placing new hardware into an existing physical machine, when a guest virtual machine is upgraded to a higher virtual hardware level, different hardware is presented, as far as the guest operating system is concerned. A best practice is to ensure that the latest version of VMware tools is installed first and then upgrade the virtual hardware. This approach ensures that any required device drivers are present, and the guest operating system can recognize the devices with minimal impact. Particularly in legacy guest operating systems, items such as network settings can disappear if the guest operating system neglects to save the existing settings and treats them as brand-new unconfigured devices.

Another consideration from the field is to take a snapshot of a virtual machine prior to a virtual machine hardware upgrade. This enables you to do a rollback in case of issues (see VMware KB 1010675).

Templates

One significant impact on a datacenter is the deployment of VMs of the same quality in a rapid fashion. Businesses no longer need to wait several days or weeks for deployment. From a design perspective, although deployment can be rapid and continuous, it must be completed correctly and as optimally as possible. A small change could affect the entire platform.

Using a template can help ensure consistency for support and operations staff, ease adding admin shares, handle known performance tweaks, batch files for known issues, and ease the support desk. In addition, the fact that all servers are logically the same build will help speed up testing for patches.

 ## Guest Virtual Machine Component Considerations

You can manage four resources within a guest VM: CPU, memory, network, and storage. You want to provide the user application sufficient resources to complete the workload in a timely fashion, without impacting other applications/tasks. Consolidation and other functionalities are desirable objectives, but you should not let these considerations distract you from the main goal: Users need their applications to work. From a platform perspective, if you provide the correct resources when required, you have done your job.

Reservations, Limits, and Shares

Every guest machine has three main performance options and a configured memory option:

- **VMX (configured memory value)**—The amount of memory or CPU presented/configured at that VM's time of creation

- **Reservation**—The amount of resources guaranteed and required to power on

- **Limit**—The maximum physical RAM allowed to be provided, if requested by the VM

- **Share value**—An indication of relative importance for the resource distribution

Based on the information gathered from the application discussions, these attributes can be configured at the guest VM level and the resource pool level.

If an application is critical and is likely to impact users if one or more of the resources are not delivered in a timely fashion, consider setting reservations for the anticipated or agreed workload. Reservations will give the guest exclusive access in the case of memory and reduce availability of time for other guests on the processors in the case of CPU reservations/contentions.

Use reservations sparingly and based on real application need. For example, it is better to reserve in exception to a known performance requirement than to reserve based on template or application minimums. The users do not care that a vSphere admin has reserved enough for 25 guest VMs running Windows 2008 R2 when the business intelligence application is not performing correctly. Are the other 24 guest VMs really needed at the same time? (If not, consider using resource pools and scheduled tasks to deal with workload variability, for example.) Thinking about the application and workload will guide a vAdmin in the right direction.

By understanding an application as much as possible, a vSphere admin can make informed decisions. Consider a server role that locks pages in memory (Java or SQL, for example). A best practice is to configure the reservation to match the allocated memory. This approach ensures the applications have full access to the memory pools as intended and prevents the hypervisor from being loaded with continuous requests.

Reservations also have an impact on shared storage. When a guest machine is powered on, the hypervisor will prepare for the worst-case scenario. By default, this scenario could potentially mean that the virtual machine has no physical memory whatsoever. An application will still need access to the files originally contained in the physical memory somewhere; therefore, a swap file per VM is created in the same size as the allocated memory minus what has been guaranteed (for example, the reservation). Unnecessarily configuring virtual machines to be larger than needed (a habit often developed in the physical world) can cause the amount of expensive shared storage wasted to be immense. You could move .vswap files to different datastores or local storage, but keep in mind that these have their own design impacts, too. See the article "(Alternative) VM Swap File Locations Q&A" from Frank Denneman's blog, at www.frankdenneman.nl, for more information.

By configuring correctly sized virtual machines according to performance and workload requirements and reserving to anticipated workloads, the amount of storage can be minimized and resource allocation guaranteed.

It can be considered a best practice to set reservations at a resource pool level for various reasons such as the fact that VMware HA is not affected (for example, the slot size value depends on the admission control policy), and attributes such as permissions and ease manageability can be factored in.

Network Considerations

Generally, a guest virtual machine is assigned a port group and configured with a network IP address. However, some key considerations can really impact a network and platform.

One consideration is how many virtual NICs to use. It is a new way of thinking to not team at the operating system level. You should handle this at the physical host layer, using teaming or active/standby ports. If existing physical machines have teams, make sure you understand which link or virtual IP addresses (if any) are used by the applications and then clean up the virtual instance using drive cleanup scripts or by re-creating interfaces.

Another key consideration is the vApp network. This is a reasonably new concept for a business. Traditionally, systems are given IP address ranges based on function, such as three VLANs for a three-tier application (for example, database VLAN, application VLAN, front-end VLAN). Multiple applications would have similar roles. Appropriate access lists created according to standardized roles are layered on top.

A vApp network can be designed to use a VLAN per application. This ensures that the hosts, which act like very smart switches for this purpose, will direct traffic between the application servers internally. Thus, if they are always running on the same vSwitch on the same host (for example, with an enforced vApp rule), the traffic between boxes and physical switches is minimized. This should also simplify troubleshooting, removing the physical interfaces from the situation (and allowing metrics such as packets in and packets out to be used easily).

Another advantage of this type of design is security. I have been asked many times about the validity of having a web-facing server and database server on the same

VLAN. However, the fact that they will talk to each other anyway would invalidate anything gained from LAN separation. This, coupled with the possible impact of a web VLAN being made vulnerable, would also give an intruder possible access to all company web-facing apps rather than just one. The original arguments against vApp network design are dwindling due to the addition of security appliances such as the VMware vShield range and vCloud Director isolated or fenced mode networks.

Storage Considerations

From a virtual machine design perspective, most of the platform work should generally have been completed prior to getting to the virtual machine layer. Here's what's left for the vSphere admin to consider:

- Install the application according to vendor best practices. If different partitions are required for different disk behavior (for example, highly read for images and read/write for database transactions), configure accordingly. Keep to one partition per underlying VMDK.

- Choose the appropriate virtual disk type.

- Align the guest VM disks according to the underlying storage. This will prevent fragmentation and wasted I/O resources.

- Determine the appropriate swap file location.

What type of virtual disk should be used? There are three main types of virtual disks to consider (but there are more than this; see VMware KB 102224):

- Thin provisioned

- Eager-zero

- Lazy-zeroed

Thin provisioning presents the guest virtual machine one capacity (for example, 100 GB) and in reality uses only what is required at the time (for example, 20 GB), allowing both flexibility by overcommitting and providing service to applications that might not be physically possible if full allocation were required. The assumption, however, is that all guest virtual machines will not require the storage allocation at the same time. Items such as test boxes can then appear to have the same specs as production machines, and so production applications can be built at much larger specs and can be moved to other platforms, if required.

The risk associated with using this type of disk in this manner is the possibility of running out of physical storage. If a datastore fills up completely, guest virtual machines running on that datastore may stop running. Thus, the risk profile is increased. Risk can be reduced with proactive monitoring using vCenter Server alarms, scripts such as the virtual vCheck script from Virtu-Al.Net, and monitoring applications.

Storage DRS is a new function in vSphere that can automatically migrate virtual machine VMDK files according to usage and other configurable rules to prevent situations such as those described previously. This function, however, is an Enterprise Plus license functionality and will not be used by all customers.

Although minimal, a performance impact might also be observed. A thin-provisioned virtual disk dynamically grows as required by the guest operating system. This growth involves three steps: a request/allocation, a block of disk being prepared for writing to (zeroing out), and then a write to disk. Clearly, with modern, fast disk systems, this may have little impact, but it is still worth a consideration.

Ideal use cases of thin-provisioned virtual disks are applications that have large static areas of data, with application I/O behavior highly read in nature rather than transactional (for example, web server images). Benchmarking the performance of thin-provisioned disks on the platform would be a helpful metric when designing a guest VM.

Thick disks have the entire allocation dedicated at the time of creation, thereby removing the risk of overcommitment, although this reduces flexibility. The difference between the two types of thick disks is the time at which the disk is ready to be written to. A lazy-zeroed VMDK file has the entire space allocated but not prepared for data (zeroed).

On an eager-zeroed disk, the area is zeroed out and prepared for data at the time of creation, therefore taking longer to deploy but, in theory, offering faster write time. In theory, highly transactional or I/O-driven applications should be configured with an eager-zeroed disk to attain the best possible write time.

Please note, however, that the performance impact of these virtual disks when used with modern disk systems may have minor impacts on users' applications. Other issues, such as flexibility and risk, might be the deciding factors. Benchmarks and actual performance would be required to make an informed decision. Understanding the vendor's requirement or the application I/O requirements is the key here.

CPU Considerations

Unlike with virtual memory allocation, a guest VM does not generally own a CPU (although it is possible with CPU affinity configuration). Each VM requests CPU resources via the VMkernel, which allocates or schedules the VM time on the appropriate processor.

Consider a host with 4 quad-core sockets installed and no hyperthreading enabled. The number of available logical CPUs is 16. This gives a maximum capacity of 16 vCPUs being executed at the same time.

It is possible to run many more than 16 VMs, thanks to CPU scheduling and guest vCPU allocation. In a predictive platform design, each VM would be allocated a number of vCPUs, and no overcommitment would be planned. In a more fluid platform, the number of VMs would be dictated by the CPU requirements of the applications running within them and whether there would be sufficient opportunities for the VMs to get ample CPU time.

One of the key questions in designing a VM for an application is whether the application is multithreaded. An application that is multithreaded can execute processes simultaneously on two separate vCPUs. An application such as this would benefit from being allocated the same number of CPUs as the number of threads it can execute.

An application that is not multithreaded could in fact be able to complete less work if it received an allocation of multiple CPUs. This outcome is due to the fact the VMkernel will consider the requests in allocated blocks. For example, if a VM asks for CPU time with four CPUs but is single threaded, the VM process will be allocated four CPU threads at the same time. However, the application will process on only one thread, thus wasting opportunities for three CPUs. If the host is busy or overcommitted, this could have a substantial effect on the effective consolidation ratio. In addition to the problem of the wasted resources, the fact that a VM is requesting four CPUs would mean it is less likely to be offered slots at a busy time. One-quarter of the CPUs would have to be available in order for the VM to get any time. If the VM were allocated one vCPU, however, when given the opportunity to schedule, nothing would be wasted, and because only one slot would be required, the VM would have more possible combinations to get CPU time.

The keys to correct vCPU allocation are understanding the application requirements, monitoring the CPU Ready and CPU Usage figures in an adaptive sizing approach, and not overcommitting in a predictive approach.

vSphere Platform-wide Considerations

A stable platform is vital for a vSphere admin. Planning and experience help ensure that the guest virtual machines are providing a consistent level of resources when required and requested.

Transparent Page Sharing (TPS) is a memory reclamation technique managed by the VMkernel. It is the function whereby active guest memory is deduplicated.

The process scans the guest virtual machine memory. Duplicated data is deleted, and memory space is released back to the platform. The process uses a copy-on-write function; if a guest VM attempts to write to a deduplicated memory block, the VMkernel makes a complete copy of the memory page.

The major benefit of TPS is the consolidation ratio increase. Operating systems can have very similar memory behavior, especially if applications are running on machines that are built in very similar ways (for example, template and role-based architecture). Once TPS has scanned the guest memory pages on stable machines, the physical hosts are put under less pressure, thus increasing the number of guests they can effectively run.

TPS is a fantastic functionality benefit from VMware, but you need to have a thorough understanding of application behavior if you're planning to use TPS extensively in capacity calculations. The VMkernel does not deduplicate large page files (greater than 2 MB) unless it is put under great pressure (for example, 94%). A lot of modern applications (such as Java-based web apps and SQL) utilize large memory pages. In designs, I do not suggest planning to use a hypervisor to such a high level of memory utilization.

Several additional design impact considerations exist when you're planning for TPS. First, consider a totally overcommitted host during workload, which is perceived normal and accepted as such. In the event of a workload increase, the applications could be potentially starved of memory resources (when all VMs ask for resources at the same time). The hypervisor then starts to use ballooning, compression, and swapping techniques, and, under extreme pressure, share values.

Another consideration is the use of a vSphere HA guest VM restart. The consolidation ratio of a running vSphere host could be greater than a host's initial capacity. Depending on the guest operating system's startup state (some large pages could actually contain all zeros and would therefore be ignored in vSphere 4.1 and above), it could take a considerable amount of time for TPS to scan all guest memory and deduplicate for the restarted VMs.

Antivirus Solutions for a vSphere Admin

The antivirus solution arena is full of applications from zero-day approaches to the classic manual updates. Which is best for the project you are working on?

A traditional approach is to create a policy server that holds the rules and definitions for the platform. Every machine has a client application installed and a rule base applied according to a grouping, such as location, role, and so on. The client application can scan files at the point of access of the guest machine or can have scheduled scans.

VDI sysadmins often experience a classic example of this traditional approach: All users are working on desktops running on a few host machines with the same physical platform. During a scheduled scan, several hundred desktops suddenly start scanning all their files at the same time. This activity causes a massive increase in I/O request and CPU consumption; in some cases, the platform will become 100% saturated and not only impact the users but disconnect them. To work around this, it is possible to keep with the traditional approach and components (for license and support knowledge reasons) but separate desktops to different physical disks and controllers to limit the impact of an I/O storm. Another workaround is to schedule scan times for groups at different times of day in the hope of minimizing impact.

The newer approach is to install a virtual machine that can communicate with the VMkernel through its API and offload the A/V processes in functional modules and complete them only once (not once per virtual machine process). This minimizes the resource requirements and eases administration. Various vendors are available for this type of product; the VMware-developed version is part of the VMware vShield range, thus completing the enterprise management components required without reducing consolidation ratios.

vApps

A vApp is a logical container of guest virtual machine objects. The use of a container provides the ability to use key management functionality, which can dramatically help a virtualized platform. Automation allows lots of VMs to be managed by fewer staff.

As shown in Figure 5-2, the website www.elasticsky.co.uk is the name of the application (vApp name). It consists of four server components (vApp objects). This vApp, from a general business-as-usual perspective, gives the vAdmin awareness that these servers are related and need to be considered as a unit. The vAdmin does not specifically need to be aware of how the application works to make decisions but will be able to understand the high-level impacts of certain machines.

Figure 5-2 A Multi-tier App Within a vApp Object in vSphere 5

In addition, using a vApp causes key functions to become available. For example, in many cases, multitier applications such as websites need to be started in a certain order; the database server contains all the objects the applications and web server roles require to function. Thus, if the database server is not functional at the time of power-on, the web server and application servers may fail.

As an on-call engineer, I have felt the pain of turning up at a datacenter shortly after a power outage. In one instance, I spent a few hours running around the racks, going to various KVM positions to start servers in a certain order; I had to wait for specific services to run before starting the next one. Not fun at all. By specifying the startup and shutdown order, you can automate this work.

In Figure 5-3, the startup order is specified. But what happens if the SQL service doesn't start or if one of the services takes an unusual amount of time to start? The elapsed time in seconds may not help as the times could vary, depending on the CPU cycles provided or what the service needs to do at each restart (for example, purge caches or reload feed caches). This may cause you to restart the servers manually once again.

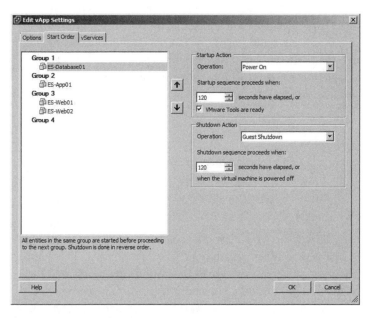

Figure 5-3   vApp Configuration for a Multitier Application

One technique for avoiding this problematic scenario is to ensure that the VMware Tools service is automatically started at startup and to make the VMware Tools services dependent on the specific application service that is required for the vApp function. (For more information see Microsoft Knowledge Base article KB193888.)

Points to Consider

DRS is required for vApp functionality to be available; the impact of this requirement is not a major aspect except in terms of costs. DRS is only included in the Enterprise and Enterprise Plus versions of the vSphere product suite.

A key design consideration is the impact on RTO when vSphere HA is invoked. Although vApps can automate startup and powerdown routines, VMware HA does not respect them at the point of failure. There are possible workarounds, using cluster startup priorities (for example, set the default priority to low, and set infrastructure virtual machines to high) and then configure application servers in a similar order. Another workaround would be to use PowerShell scripting and stop and start vApps using cmdlets following an outage. At present, automated solutions can be problematic in a large multi-app platform. For applications to return to service, manual intervention is required, and this is worth noting in a design document for operations staff to cover after a HA event.

OVFs

OVFs (Open Virtualization Format) are prepackaged virtual machines that can be created with attributes such as EULA, IP settings, and so on. They can be imported into most modern virtualization hypervisors, not just VMware, thus enabling businesses to deploy and share applications simply by importing and exporting files, as opposed to going through a long, complicated installation process.

You can create basic DR objectives or test dev systems by exporting an existing VM from a vCenter. This small function can provide massive impact to business processes. For example, consider a company that has outsourced its software development department to another country, while keeping platform and testing business functions in-house. By building standardized virtual machines and exporting them as OVFs with the out-of-box experience configured, the departments can work legally with their own licenses but with a consistent image. They can also avoid long setup and troubleshooting routines throughout the software development life cycle.

"Can I just have a new standard VM, please?" Thanks to the existence of templates and the ability to quickly deploy guest operating systems, it is very easy to get lost in the actual purpose of the vSphere platform: to host your users' application workloads.

The guest VMs are the media that actually interact with users, and they deserve at least a conversation with the vendor, developer, or user to understand how an application should behave when deployed. Documenting those conversations is also handy for troubleshooting.

Understanding how an application behaves (for example, memory driven, lots of random writes, CPU driven) will give a VMware architect an opportunity to increase workload consolidation and maintain a stable platform by making informed decisions based on maximizing the effectiveness of VMware technology functions.

Exam Preparation Tasks

Review All Key Topics

Review the most important topics in the chapter, noted with the key topics icon in the outer margin of the page. Table 5-2 lists these key topics and the page number on which each is found.

Table 5-2   Key Topics

Key Topic Element	Description	Page
List and Figure 5-1	Guest virtual machine design thoughts	105
Paragraph	Impact of resource allocation on guest virtual machine design	110

Design Scenario

Design your own vApp to support a multitier application:

- Imagine that your company is going to virtualize a new application.

- The system consists of multiple server roles and will be used by the whole company at different times of day.

  1. Create a logical application diagram that shows the server roles and data flow.

  2. Highlight the application's dependencies.

  3. List the metrics and key questions that need to be answered to define the resources. Create a checklist from this information.

  4. Create a guest virtual machine configuration for each role. Highlight options such as reservation, number of CPUs, and so on.

  5. Create a table that shows allocated resources and consumed resources for CPU, memory, and storage.

  6. Create a vApp configuration plan. Specify startup order and power-off order.

  7. List the assumptions you have made to establish the configuration.

Define Key Terms

Define the following key terms from this chapter and check your answers in the glossary.

vApp, CPU Ready, OVF

Review Questions

The answers to these review questions are in Appendix A.

1. You have been asked to design a virtual machine for a new application developed in-house. The application will be load tested before it is finally made production ready. The application developers have created documentation based on data flow and entity dependency. The functionality of the application is critical to the business for a defined project with a client base of a maximum of 12,000 users. Which of the following scaling approaches would best suit this scenario?

    a. Predictive

    b. Adaptive

2. You are a virtualization consultant at a company that develops its own in-house website trading systems. The new website will be deployed in a vSphere 5 platform, which consists of two clusters and four ESXi hosts (one for each project—the SDLC hosts—for all levels of testing and development prior to production deployment).

    The production cluster has been configured for fully automated DRS and VMware HA. During the SDLC, the website platform was developed on a single development ESXi host inside a single VLAN. The system was successfully tested within the SDLC ESXi hosts and then deployed to the production cluster in a single vApp and a single VLAN.

    Following a successful midweek, the new application starts to show signs of latency. Suddenly several applications across the cluster are being impacted by network latency issues. Metrics are collected and show that the amount of network traffic between the database and application servers of the new website platform are at 96% utilization on the physical switch links between ESXi hosts in the production cluster. What should you do?

   a. Recommend that the website platform be fixed and removed from the production system.

   b. Create a DRS affinity rule to ensure that the database and applications servers stay on the same ESXi host and do not traverse the physical network when communicating.

   c. Configure Network I/O Control to ensure that the network latency is alleviated between the database and applications servers.

Question Scenario

You are working on a project to deploy a critical multitier web application. The application is as follows:

Number of Servers	Server Role	Memory Allocation	CPU Allocation	Disk Allocation
20	Web	8 GB	2 vCPU	80 GB system, 150 GB data
5	Processing	2 GB	2 vCPU	80 GB system, 50 GB data
2	Database	32 GB	8 vCPU	80 GB system, 300 GB logs, 500 GB data

   3. In the scenario described, the SAN space is limited. Which of the following options would help save space while still providing the infrastructure shown above?

   a. Confirm that 80 GB is actually used on the servers in each tier and configure thin provisioning to save space.

   b. Reduce the amount of memory in each web server by 2 GB to reduce the amount of swap space created.

   c. Create a resource pool hierarchy for the web, processing, and database tiers in the application and configure a reservation for the total amount in each tier. This would reduce the amount of space used within the datastore.

4. In the scenario described, which of the following would be a good design choice for memory management in the vSphere platform?

   a. Configure each web server in the application to have a limit of 4 GB. Create a business-as-usual task to monitor the usage and increase it as required.

   b. Configure a DRS affinity rule to split 50% of the web servers between two hosts.

   c. Configure web servers to have high share values.

5. In the scenario described, which of the following would be a good alternate design choice to discuss with the vendor/web development team?

   a. Consider consolidating the database servers into one large server for ease of management, backup, and licensing costs.

   b. Consider creating a file server with UNC file shares presenting the read-only data for web servers. This would reduce the amount of space required from approximately 3 TB to approximately 150 GB.

   c. Reduce the specifications of each web server and increase the number of servers to distribute the load more widely across the cluster.

This chapter covers the following subjects:

- **Implementation Approach and Order of Delivery:** This section explains the importance of the order in which phases are carried out and the impact to the business project objectives.

- **Validation, Thoughts, and Processes:** This section discusses what types of tests and processes should be carried out to ensure that a platform is implemented and configured correctly.

- **Documentation and Delivery:** This section covers the supporting documentation required for project execution and validation.

This chapter covers the following objectives of the VCAP5-DCD blueprint:

Objective 4.1, "Create and execute a validation plan"

Objective 4.2, "Create an implementation plan"

Objective 4.3, "Create an installation guide"

CHAPTER 6

Project Execution

A project methodology is extremely useful in helping a designer get started. Gathering information and asking good questions are great skills. What about the approach? The order in which the vision is accomplished can, in some projects, be as important as the task itself.

Depending on what stage of the project life cycle a designer works within or up to, different documentation and levels of detail may be required.

A designer may create design documentation, own a product, and ensure correct platform governance but never actually log on or build the components. Clear and comprehensive implementation and installation documentation is, therefore, of great importance to ensure that the final solution delivered matches the logical and physical designs.

"Do I Know This Already?" Quiz

The "Do I Know This Already?" quiz allows you to assess whether you should read this entire chapter or simply jump to the "Exam Preparation Tasks" section for review. If you are in doubt, read the entire chapter. Table 6-1 outlines the major headings in this chapter and the corresponding "Do I Know This Already?" quiz questions. You can find the answers in Appendix A, "Answers to the 'Do I Know This Already?' and Chapter Review Questions."

Table 6-1 "Do I Know This Already?" Foundation Topics Section-to-Question Mapping

Foundations Topics Section	Questions Covered in This Section
Implementation Approach and Order of Delivery	6
Validation, Thoughts, and Processes	1, 2, 5, 7
Documentation and Delivery	3, 4, 8–10

1. CPU Ready is a metric that indicates the amount of time it takes to provide requested CPU resources to a specific virtual machine.

    a. True

    b. False

2. A validation plan should contain tests based on which of the following?

    a. Application performance experience

    b. Platform performance statistics

    c. Both a and b

3. A validation plan should contain summary configuration information for both virtual machines and host machines.

    a. True

    b. False

4. A validation plan should contain several types of workloads to show platform performance during normal business usage (for example, low, medium, high).

    a. True

    b. False

5. Application performance test cases should be based on what?

    a. Quantitative success criteria

    b. Qualitative success criteria

6. An implementation plan considers the order of the tasks/phases in which they are completed and relates them to business objectives.

    a. True

    b. False

7. Planned guest virtual machine placement using DRS rules can increase overall server consolidation and reduce resource contention.

    a. True

    b. False

8. Which of the following should an implementation plan contain?

    a. A detailed list of tasks and process for each phase of a project

    b. A summary of tasks in each phase of a project, with links to supporting documentation for further information

9. An installation guide should contain entry and exit criteria.

   a. True

   b. False

10. An installation guide should contain basic troubleshooting and baseline monitoring information, if it is useful for verification purposes.

    a. True

    b. False

Foundation Topics

Implementation Approach and Order of Delivery

Recently I was working for a large enterprise that had brought in a new CTO and hoped to stabilize and develop the IT function for the business. This involved a large virtualization project.

The first part of my role was to establish information and build an understanding of the current infrastructure. Once I had a list of tasks, I was tempted to go plowing into the project.

The vision of the project was "Any service, Anywhere." The project essentially needed a private, large-scale lab network with various applications; the enterprise wanted to make this network available in a flexible and secure manner. However, this was not the only requirement. The vision also called for a datacenter migration and P2V phase. "Anywhere access" was required by a certain date, in addition to DR considerations. This vision posed a wonderful technical challenge; however, the task was daunting in its magnitude and potential failure points.

After the information gathering stage, the tasks were highlighted, and a phased approach was devised:

1. Virtualization platform implementation

2. VDI implementation

3. vCloud implementation

4. Datacenter migration

The order of implementation in this project was vital to its success.

The key issues were as follows:

- The current building was to be demolished in 6 months' time.

- The new office was separate from the datacenter.

- The new lab was insecure with regard to key passes and so on.

- Additional application workloads were required during the project life cycle (affecting capacity planning and network complexity due to extra network requirements).

- The existing platform's hardware support had expired.

- Virtualization of the user workloads and introducing virtual desktops replacing the users' laptops had previously failed due to poor implementation. End users would need to be engaged with the project as early as possible.

- The new datacenter/office was not available until 6 weeks before the company was to move in.

Establishing the Order of Delivery

Considering the extensive list of issues involved, a delivery time of 6 months seemed tight but realistic. The vision might not be fully delivered at that point; however, the time constraint of the current office building being demolished demanded a stable platform for the users to work on. Temporary physical local machines would also not be suitable due to lack of secure areas in the new building. VDI was required in a stable, secure form on day 1 in the new office.

The lack of a change freeze could be also problematic: Capacity planning would be hard to gauge. (Initial workloads analyzed and used to build the new datacenter platform might not have been a true representation of the actual workloads in use just before the actual move.)

 ### Technical Approach

The approach taken in this project was to build a new VMware environment intended for the new datacenter at the existing site within the infrastructure. Once validated as a suitable platform, all new applications were deployed into the new platform.

The VDI implementation was developed in such a way that all new applications were available only through this medium, thus testing and giving users confidence in the technology. The process allowed new technology and applications to be created.

Information and capacity planning techniques were carried out on existing physical kits, which allowed a planned and safe P2V process to be created.

Over a period of 4 months, the new platform was developed to provide function while remaining minimal in size (and therefore easy to move). The modular vSphere platform was created to house the applications. Six weeks before the users moved in, I was granted access to the new building, which was still under construction, so that I could install the minimal vSphere platform layer in the new datacenter.

Thanks to storage replication and a dedicated point-to-point link, the existing virtual machines were continuously replicated, and the applications were tested at the new datacenter as fit for purpose.

The weekend of the actual move occurred 3 weeks prior to demolition of the old buildings. By that point, all users were already comfortable with the use of VDI access. All applications had been tested previously in the new datacenter by bringing up temporary versions of the machines.

The weekend of the move saw us turning off all machines at the old site and turning on machines at the new site and also giving access to key users to finally validate applications for going live.

Once validation occurred, the DNS entry for the VDI connection servers was flipped to the new datacenter, and all services were brought online.

Users appeared on Monday morning with a new building but no change in technology or access route. The old site was now redundant. In some cases, users could work from home and wait to settle in. The secure applications were now accessible anywhere via VDI.

Replication was flipped in the other direction, allowing a failback if needed. Once senior management was happy that data and application migration were successful, replication was stopped. The old site data was deleted, and we carried out a simple lift and shift to the new datacenter; we integrated usable components with additional modules in the new datacenter vSphere platform.

This approach satisfied all requirements and minimized risk at each stage. Another advantage of this approach was that by logically building a new site/datacenter, a DR process had already been created and tested in theory. Templates and documentation were created for this. The final phase, once users were working, was to copy the templates and use the DR documentation to create a failover site at a vCloud provider. Based on the preceding project phases, this was a relatively easy task and posed no risk to current work.

The project vision could have been completed in several other ways. All the alternatives risked impact to users and had the potential to stall the project at various phases, potentially meaning waiting for other dependencies to come online.

In all projects, various tasks can be listed and carried out in different orders. If you judge the impacts and dependencies of the tasks involved in a project, you can think through the implementation order. Personally, I prefer an agile delivery method whereby small modular deliverables are produced for the business and reviewed. This allows the business to gain confidence in the approach and, in return, provide feedback to the project team. There are other project methodologies, too. For example, the waterfall approach is a highly regimented tactic whereby requirements and documentation are created for each stage, and then final product is released.

Validation, Thoughts, and Processes

Going live is an exciting time, especially in a large project. This is the point at which all your hard work has been focused. How can you tell whether the project will be a success?

In the information gathering phase, it is important to establish requirements for the design approach and also for validating the final product.

A validation plan can range from a detailed test plan to high-level statements. Neither should be subjective.

The best validation is to place a platform under a typical test of what it will be faced with in the field—for example, having a simulated number of users go through a workflow (perhaps a website). A lot of these tasks vary with the type of application and are primarily application functionality based. In addition, platform or infrastructure metrics are key for validation and for information to be used within the operational documentation (for example, troubleshooting guide, monitoring recommendations).

VMware platforms have four main resources that can be managed. During an allocated test period, monitoring key metrics will enable the project to be validated. Table 6-2 lists the validation metrics.

Table 6-2 Validation Metrics

Resource	Metric
CPU	%READY and Average Consumed CPU
Memory	Ballooning, Compression, Swap in, and Swap Out
Network	Packets In and Packets Out
Storage	Queue Length, Physical Device Latency, VMkernel Latency, and Guest Operating System Queue Length

In addition to these metrics, application-driven platform acceptance criteria, such as the time it takes for a user registration or a page to be rendered, should also be used.

When you create a virtualized platform for a specific business application, it is possible to just send an email over to the users saying "Done" and wait for the inevitable cry "This isn't working!" or "It seems a little slow." A more problematic scenario is when a system has been tested and seemingly accepted by the users, but you find that a few days, weeks, or months later, a crucial component is missing.

Establishing a thorough and fair test is critical and should involve a high-level test plan with agreed tests based on application functionality. From a VMware platform perspective, it would be helpful to include expected results or acceptable criteria for sign-off.

There are two main test objectives from the platform perspective.

- **Design verification**—Validate that the design and configuration actually work as intended. For example, when considering the structure of a multitier web store, users browse a catalog of items, log in and buy items, then log out.

- **Operational testing**—Ensure that the technical solution provides an acceptable user experience and meets expectations from all stakeholder types. For example, a website is functional, responsive with regard to page rendering times, and easy to upgrade and support.

Table 6-3 provides an example of a test plan.

Table 6-3 An Example of a Test Plan

Test Case ID	Test information	Expected Results	Actual Results	Pass/Fail	Notes
Plat001	Load balancer functionality Requires users from 3 different test locations Log in to URL. Select 3 items and add to basket. Ensure server status using hidden server. txt file.	Users distributed according to weighted round robin (check load balancer stats). Once user has logged in successfully, remain on specified server. Basket contents consistent until purchase.			

Test Case ID	Test information	Expected Results	Actual Results	Pass/Fail	Notes
Plat002	During test period, disable VMware tools on web server at random.	Load balancer disables affected web server from web farm. VMware HA restart web server using virtual machine monitoring feature. Confirm screenshot.			
Plat003					

A useful process when considering solutions is to ensure that the infrastructure qualities are considered at each phase (refer to Chapter 3, "Thoughts on Good Choices for Virtualization and Design"). Doing so ensures that the major attributes are at least thought about.

Various tools are useful in creating loads for testing or benchmarking. These tools can be used in several ways:

- Stress, capacity, and load testing to simulate representative workloads or test to failure

- Physical to virtual comparisons, including quantitative stats of virtual versus physical machines

- Monitoring and gathering useful information during workloads for troubleshooting, operational guides, and validation.

You can normally answer the layperson's classic question of how much slower is VMware than a physical machine by establishing the application requirements (new application deployments) or by baselining the existing physical platform with key workloads and showing that these workloads are easily supportable.

A vSphere admin needs to show that the fact that the system is running in a virtualized platform is actually insignificant to the end user. The application will work as intended, both logically and physically.

As mentioned in VCP level study, there are four manageable resources: CPU, memory, network, and storage. These key components can be distributed to the guest virtual machines. A vSphere admin needs to help ensure that applications have the correct amount of each of these resources within a time suitable for the application in order for the end user to deem the application usable.

An engineer will have plenty of experience in troubleshooting performance issues. This experience can be utilized at a different stage of the application life cycle to help ensure correct implementation. In my project example, one of the key applications had previously failed in a virtualized implementation. End users were saying things like "We have to go physical with this one!" and "VMware doesn't work with demanding applications." Forgetting the office politics, this application was a requirement for the migration. A successful implementation was achieved through the following process:

1. Talking to the SMEs on the specialized application

2. Establishing understanding of the logic of the application

3. Ensuring vendor support and licensing in a virtualization platform is possible/available

4. Converting (P2V) the platform

5. Testing the platform on each logical phase of the application

6. Comparing results

This process could be seen as a mini-project; all the phases are there. The main project at a high level may only list this application as being in scope, with very little information. On further investigation, aspects such as failed virtualized implementation would be brought to light. In this particular situation, by discussing the application logically, I discovered that the application consisted of two roles:

- A licensing server

- A processing server

Both servers were in fact "monster" servers for the time when they were purchased, with over 200 GB RAM, 16 threads of CPU, and four 1 GB NICs. The logic of the application was such that the licensing server was only a beacon, which was perfect and easy for a P2V process. As long as the processing server could communicate over a specific TCP port to the licensing server, the application was operational.

The behavior of the processing server was slightly different; its function was split into three phases:

1. The application copies the project data under investigation (possibly terabytes) and places it into custom databases spread across the server's physical data drives.

2. The data is read in a sequential manner, and relevant information from search parameters is stored in active memory.

3. Useful data links are exported as a file and database for relationship modeling.

How do you approach an application such as this? It is possible that a straight P2V may not work in this case for several reasons:

- The size of the data the application contains and its rate of change if the system is in continuous use could be problematic. The P2V may be impractical to clone within a certain time frame; it may never finish.

- It could have a great impact on the network or other workloads. For example, interdependent components, such as core switch interfaces or bandwidth availability, could be affected by copying such a large amount of data across the enterprise network the systems use.

- Phase 1 requires as much network traffic as possible to copy the data and then disk I/O to write the data to the required locations.

- Phase 2 uses high disk I/O, CPU, and memory to process the search parameters and load them into the memory.

- Phase 3 uses large amounts of memory, and although it requires a small amount of disk I/O, it has a very low tolerance for disk latency.

The approach taken to virtualize this platform was first to analyze the hardware under normal processing workloads. In talking to the SMEs, I asked for a standard project size and the largest project size to determine the workload parameters. The acceptable time and actual time for processing these amounts of workload data were also noted. This gave the expected performance criteria.

As long as the virtualized version of this application's performance was comparable to that of the physical version, within the acceptable time parameters, the application would be successfully implemented. It is best to have these parameters (entry and exit criteria) agreed with the business or referred to as an assumption in your high-level document (for example, business growth may affect this by a percentage).

The following key metrics were monitored while processing the workloads:

- **CPU**—Average, Peak, and Minimum (MHz)

- **Memory**—Usage: Average, Peak, and Minimum (MB)

- **Network**—Average, Peak, and Minimum (MB, Packets Received/ Transmitted)

- **Storage**—Average IOPS Read/Write, Disk Queue Length

Once these metrics were collected, the guest platform was designed. A simple P2V of the processing server was taken to obtain the installation, and following guest design changes, the workloads were retested.

In addition to the physical metrics, the following VMware metrics were noted:

- **CPU**—CPU Ready and CPU Wait Time
- **Memory**—Ballooning, Shared Memory, Compression, Paging, and Swapping
- **Network**—Host Utilization and VM Utilization
- **Storage**—Read Latency and Write Latency

Combining both the physical and virtual metrics and comparing them with regard to user expectations was extremely useful. This validation process allowed quantitative assurance to prove that the application was or was not performing as required.

An interesting issue in this project was the failure of phase 3, where memory and I/O were required at the export function. Although at this stage the memory and CPU requirements were nowhere near the maximum, the application was written in such a way that there was very little tolerance to memory latency (that is, there was a very low timeout value). Thus, if the application didn't get the 64 GB of memory exactly at the time it needed to, the whole process crashed. The application was not logically tolerant; therefore, the entire process on the workload had to be repeated. The typical workload took 36 hours to complete, which was a significant setback for the project.

Phase 3 was, in fact, the point where the first virtual implementation failed. However, armed with the relevant metrics, it was easy to set a reservation (either on the specific workload VM or at resource pool level) to 64 GB memory. This guaranteed the memory available at the time of export and the workload completed. (The memory was available right away, and the process completed within the timeout value.)

After logical success, the workloads were rerun to establish that the system was reliable and to gain understanding of the behavior of the application and the hosts supporting it. Both the virtual and physical metrics were noted and referenced in the operations guide for second-line support.

Going Live and the Bedding-in Period

The application example discussed in this chapter was one of many applications within a larger project. Due to its criticality, the application had a highly demanding SLA in many regards. The application was released to end users via VDI access, but the vSphere admin's job didn't stop there.

Due to the aggregation of resources in VMware platforms, applications can have dependencies on each other that are not apparent. A finance application, for example, may have a high workload at the same time as another critical application in another department.

It is important to consider the requirements of all the applications at varied workloads in totality. For example, do production applications hit peak workloads at similar times or overlapping times? At these points, does the platform have sufficient capability to provide adequate resources for the applications?

Functions such as DRS, memory and CPU reservations, limits, shares, Network I/O Control (NIOC), and profile-driven storage can be used to alleviate possible bottleneck. Including any of these functions may, however, add complexity to the overall design.

From a design perspective, other strategies could be integrated, such as server placement. In the example discussed here, phase 1 uses substantial network bandwidth and copies all data from a virtual file server to the processing server. It could be beneficial to have the servers (that is, the processing server and corresponding file source) used in phase 1 in the same network and to ensure that DRS rules are configured to have both roles always on the same physical host. This configuration should remove the requirement to have network traffic leave the physical host during phase 1 and reduce bandwidth contention and impact on other applications.

However useful tweaks and performance considerations are, when allowing for future growth, it may be better to consider increasing host resource capacity.

Documentation and Delivery

Documentation requirements vary from enterprise to enterprise. Depending on an individual's job specification, a single designer or consultant could be the main creator and user of documentation at different points in the project life cycle. The primary roles of documentation in situations like this are to help guide the project process, to ensure that knowledge transfer can take place at any time, and to validate the project after it is delivered (providing evidence of the design processes, for due diligence, and for peer review).

More detailed documentation may be required if multiple teams are involved. A designer who did not actually implement the solution would still be required to include sufficient detail in documentation information to enable the engineering or build team to implement the solution as intended (with validation steps to effectively prove the completeness of the project).

As a high-level design does not normally detail physical hardware or specific configuration, an installation guide or some type of low-level design guide is required.

In addition, in medium to large projects where tasks have been grouped into phases, it is important to ensure that all members of the project team complete the tasks in the intended manner and at the correct times.

Implementation Plans

An implementation plan provides all members of a project team with a level of understanding of the technical approach of a project, the number of phases, major tasks in each phase, and the correct order for completing them.

This documentation can be used to bring in skilled people and to judge the project stability and progress throughout the implementation. The plan should be detailed enough for technical personnel to understand the tasks being completed but without specific configuration and installation processes being detailed. The following are examples of sections to include in an implementation plan:

- Overview of the project

- Important contact information (key personnel, vendor support information)

- List of phases and major tasks in each phase

- Risks and assumptions and dependencies to phases being implemented

- Order and schedule of implementation

- Highlighted dependencies and milestones

- Reference to supporting documentation, such as a high-level design, physical designs, and installation guides

Installation Guides

An installation guide provides engineers a detailed reference and process to install and verify a solution. All relevant components and processes are detailed. It is also useful to include troubleshooting or known issues if any were experienced during the development and test phases.

Key entry and exit criteria should be detailed to ensure that the person carrying out the installation understands what is required and when the process is complete.

Although the contents and style may vary from company to company, an installation guide should normally contain the following:

- Overview or summary of the purpose of the guide/technology

- Configuration diagrams and explanations of the platform, environment, or application

- Entry criteria and exit criteria

- Installation procedures (run sheet/run books) for tasks or links to supporting documentation

- Verification process

- Troubleshooting steps and known issues

For an IT professional, automation is power! Machines are generally very good at completing a repeatable process very quickly and in the same manner each time. A skilled engineer and designer can take advantage of this and create scripts or utilize automated vSphere platform functions, such as Host Profiles, Auto Deploy, and vSphere Distributed Switches (VDS).

A highly complex design can be implemented very simply, using blocks of automating functions or scripts. vSphere is a highly modular platform, with numerous tools to make configuration and administration as easy as possible (for example, Power-CLI, vMA, Onyx, vCenter Orchestrator, Auto Deploy, Host Profile).

An installation guide could contain step-by-step instructions on how to configure each component. Presenting such a guide is time consuming, requires verification via peer review, and then needs to be factored into implementation plans and time lines. Alternatively, the installation guide could include a selection of automation scripts and references to supporting documentation.

These automation scripts, when executed under detailed environment entry criteria, could build the platform extremely quickly. Separate validation scripts could be run to ensure that the process has completed correctly. The installation document could, therefore, at this stage be a lot simpler, and the skill set of the engineer does not need to be as specialized.

Automation in this way could have a positive effect on the implementation plan, reducing the time to deploy each phase and the overall project duration. In theory, the risk of configuration error should be substantially less, assuming that the scripts were validated correctly. In addition, the use of automation scripts could be added to a DR plan whereby the system is built quickly, allowing lower RTO and RPO levels.

A decision should be made about whether an operations guide is required, with business-as-usual tasks such as patching, monitoring, and expansion of the platform detailed.

Exam Preparation Tasks

Review All Key Topics

Review the most important topics in the chapter, noted with the key topics icon in the outer margin of the page. Table 6-4 lists these key topics and the page number on which each is found.

Table 6-4   Key Topics

Key Topic Element	Description	Page
Paragraph	Impact of technical approach and implementation order	128
Table 6-2	Validation metrics	130
List	Documentation required	137

Design Scenario

You are a virtualization consultant working in a large enterprise. You have been tasked to lead a significant server consolidation project. One of the 15 user-critical applications is a multitier web-based application that is used by both internal and external end users. The application consists of 18 servers, and there are four server roles:

- Web server (currently 6 production servers behind a physical load balancer)

- Application server (3 production servers)

- Database server (2 production servers; mirrored SQL 2008)

- File server (holding native user data; 3 servers in production with 19 TB of native data)

The CTO has attended a design workshop meeting with various other stakeholders. The following are key points from the meeting:

- The current system is not performing as required by the business for current workloads.

- The business is working toward a virtual-first strategy. The aim is to complete all critical applications within 8 months.

- The number of projects will double within 6 months.

- The software vendor has not virtualized this system before. However, it has dedicated time with your client to work to complete this process successfully.

- The business is now shifting all production work to this vendor solution. Therefore, the SLA has changed to uptime of 99.9% per year, RTO of 4 hours, and RPO of 15 minutes.

Complete the following tasks:

1. Draw a logical diagram of the application.

2. Annotate the diagram, showing the relationships between the components (for example, upstream and downstream).

3. Write out the infrastructure qualities and add at least three key points for consideration, based on the diagrams drawn in tasks 1 and 2.

4. Based on the diagrams, create a list of high-level tasks to achieve the project vision. Separate them into phases and consider the order in which to complete the phases. Make a note of what skills are required at what times.

5. Create a table similar to the example shown here. Consider validation tests and expected results.

Test Case ID	Test Information	Expected Results	Actual Results	Pass/Fail	Notes
Plat001					

As part of these tasks, you do the following:

- Create a high-level logical diagram and component relationship diagram

- Consider infrastructure qualities during a design process

- Create a validation plan

- Create an implementation plan

Definitions of Key Terms

Define the following key terms from this chapter and check your answers in the glossary.

Validation plan, Implementation plan, Entry criteria, Exit criteria

Review Questions

The answers to these review questions are in Appendix A.

1. Entry criteria should be included in all areas of documentation designed for implementation and validation.

    a. True

    b. False

2. A validation plan should be based on estimated workloads and user behavior.

    a. True

    b. False

3. A validation plan is used to do which of the following? (Select all that apply.)

    a. Verify the design

    b. Verify that the system is functional

    c. Verify that the system meets requirements

    d. Meet current best practices

4. vSphere cluster functionality such as DRS and HA does not need to be part of a validation plan. This kind of documentation is only concerned with guest VM workload validation, not platform-wide validation.

    a. True

    b. False

5. The technical approach and order of delivery can have an impact on which of the following? (Select all that apply.)

    a. Overall delivery time

    b. People resource contention (right person, right time, right task)

    c. Validation phase duration

This chapter covers the following subjects:

- **Final Preparation Tasks:** Studying for the test and real-life designing
- **A Review of the VCAP5-DCD Exam:** A VCAP5-DCD experience

CHAPTER 7

Tips For Passing The Exam

The VCAP5-DCD exam is a difficult but very passable certification. I have taken both versions 4 and 5; on neither occasion did I leave the exam room thinking they were easy, nor did I feel the questions were unfair. If you study carefully, you can pass the exam.

The challenge I found with the test is that it is extremely long. Nearly four hours of staring at a computer screen in a semi-stressed exam state is not my idea of fun. In this chapter I provide tips to help you pass the exam.

The Blueprint

Examine the blueprint and ensure that you understand all the objectives. This book covers the principles of those objectives.

Read the documentation highlighted in this book, but don't spend time memorizing random facts.

I have read and to some extent agree with blogs which suggest that you either know the information you need for the VCAP5-DCD exam or you don't. If you have plenty of design experience, understand vSphere technology, and have a working knowledge of IT, I would expect you to pass.

For example, you're a third-line engineer who has recently completed a VCP, but you have little or no real-life datacenter design experience? Never fear; you can pass the exam, but you will need to do a substantial amount of background reading.

A VCP-level certification is a prerequisite qualification and is therefore a good reference point for the level of knowledge required to pass the VCAP5-DCD exam. The types of questions in the two exams are similar in that you could be given real-life scenarios involving a VMware platform. However, on the VCAP5-DCD exam, the VMware knowledge in most questions is pretty much assumed, and you need to think about the impact rather than a specific fact or setting.

For example, a VCP exam question might be "In vSphere 5, VMware HA uses a master/slave topology and can withstand network partitioning. True or false?" A VCAP-level question, on the other hand, might present a company's intention to use VMware HA as a disaster-recovery tool, and you would be given the specifications of the servers used in the platform. The objective of the question would be to create a high-level HA design, including specifying the number of servers that would be required to support the platform, according to best practice. Both levels of questioning require knowledge of the topology and an understanding of the use cases and practical limitations of VMware HA. However, the VCAP-level question assumes that you know the facts, have designed to best practices in real life, and therefore will create the expected design.

If you are a break fix engineer, your hands-on knowledge is invaluable for configuration settings and such. However, understanding when and how to use certain design choices may be your particular learning curve and is something you must develop by reading case studies and applying design methodologies. For more information, see Chapter 1, "Introduction to Technical Design"; Chapter 2, "Creating a Design"; and Chapter 3, "Thoughts on Good Choices for Virtualization and Design."

Studying for the Test and Real-Life Designing

Due to the content of the blueprint and how the exam questions are created, it would be impractical to discuss all possible design choices and best practices for the vSphere platform. Basically, you should ensure that you complete the design documentation detailed at the end of each chapter of this book (in the section "Exam Preparation Tasks"). You should also have a process for designing each vSphere component.

When you have a design process you are comfortable with and understand what documentation and design choices you may be required to work with, consider the content highlighted in Appendix B, "Recommended Reading and Assumed Platform Knowledge." This will give you an understanding of popular best practices and reference materials for future real-life design work.

The Exam Design Tool

In the VCAP5-DCD exam, several questions require you to construct a logical or physical high-level design drawing. You accomplish this by using a design tool.

To help you prepare, VMware has released a video demo of this tool on the mylearn.vmware.com website. It is very easy to use, and I have found it to be very responsive. This tool is similar to a Microsoft Visio diagram, with a scenario description and an area for the candidate to construct or finish a logical or physical diagram for a proposed solution (see Figure 7-1).

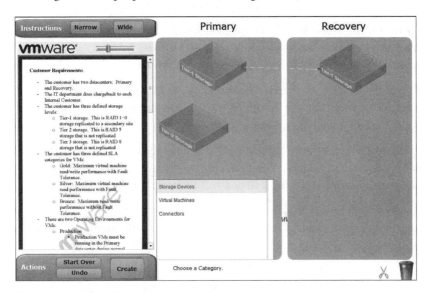

Figure 7-1   The VMware Design User Interface

Tips for E-design Tool Questions

E-design tool questions can be scary and potentially time-consuming to answer, especially when they feature an unfamiliar tool. The keys here are to apply VMware technology in an appropriate way and to keep the design simple.

Read through the design guidance in the question. It will help you understand how to construct the diagram. For example, say that you are asked to design a storage solution for a company using fibre-channel storage. The tool will only offer relevant objects for selection; for example, Storage Array, Storage Processor, and Switch.

Lay out the required number of components, based on the scenario, and connect them together using the connector objects. The design guidance will tell you which connectors to use and in what order they are required. Remember that redundancy and the direction of the arrows can matter.

My VCAP5-DCD Experience

I took the VCAP5-DCD exam about three weeks after its release. I thought it would be worth including a few words on my experience of the exam here.

You can register for the test at www.pearsonvue/VMware. The exam is one of the advanced-level VMware certifications, and authorization from VMware is required before you can book an exam date. This process takes a few days.

Only a few test centers are authorized to hold the VCAP exam. In my case, I was lucky as an available center was just 10 minutes away from my workplace, but you need to be prepared for a wait or traveling.

When I arrived at the test center, I went through an enhanced security check: photograph, removal of my watch, removal of the contents of my pockets, and so on. Keep in mind that this is a long exam, and you will be busy. The exam is as much a test of physical endurance as a test of your knowledge!

You will face 100 questions, mainly multiple choice, with a small number of actual design questions using the design tool mentioned earlier. After you answer each question, you are unable to go back and review it.

Each design tool question took me approximately 10 minutes or so to complete. The wording and the tasks sometimes didn't quite flow for me. I found the design guidance more useful, but I more or less ignored the scenario, except for a quick glance and read through the text to look for applicable requirements. The objects that were available to me in the tool also gave me a nice tip on what I should be drawing and also limited my design. (I'm guessing this is the idea.)

I completed the exam with only 10 minutes to spare—phew! The score appeared promptly at the end of the test, and, thankfully, I was successful. I have taken dozens of certification exams over the past few years, and I would say that the VCAP exams (with the exception of vendor defenses, such as the VCI) are the most thorough. They are also the most rewarding.

Good luck with your VCAP5-DCD exam. I hope you find this guide useful. I would be very happy to hear from anyone who wants to say "hello" or provide feedback on this book or VCAP exam experiences. You can reach me at my website, www.elasticsky.co.uk.

Exam Preparation Tasks

Final Preparation Tasks

Consider a project you have worked on. Write a two-page summary HLD, with these headings:

- Requirements

- Constraints

- Assumptions

- Logical Design of Network, Storage, Compute, Management Components

- Sample Physical Design of Network, Storage, and Compute Components

- vApp Design and High-Level Cluster Settings

- Dependencies from the User to the Service

- DR, RTO, and RPO Considerations

This summary can serve as your final review guide. You can also use it as a template for real-life projects. I use such summaries during real design walkthroughs and workshops to help ensure that I have covered the main considerations.

Please see my website, www.elasticsky.co.uk/dcdguide, for the latest resources and examples of these tasks.

Real-Life Tips from Field and Design Defenses

- Apply the knowledge you have gained from the certification study, but amend it for each project.

- Create your own template documents. Using them for even mini-projects will help with larger implementations and in design meetings and workshops.

- Have a summary HLD on hand. Also, with application considerations, have a data flow diagram prepared for walkthrough of communication.

- Know the design. You need to understand how you got there, what justifies the design choices you have made, and what risks are associated with the agreed approach. All designs will have an element of this; each project is a balancing act tailored for the business objective.

- Understand your audience (for example, techie or nontechie).

Answers to the "Do I Know This Already?" Quizzes and Chapter Review Questions

"Do I Know This Already?" Answers

Chapter 1

1. B
2. C
3. A
4. B
5. A
6. B
7. B
8. B
9. A
10. A
11. A
12. B
13. A

Chapter 2

1. A
2. A
3. C
4. A
5. C
6. A

7. A
8. A
9. A
10. C

Chapter 3

1. B
2. B
3. B
4. A
5. C
6. B
7. A
8. A
9. A
10. D

Chapter 4

1. A
2. A
3. B
4. B

5. C

6. B

7. B

8. A

9. A

10. B

11. A

12. C

13. D

14. B

15. A

Chapter 5

1. A

2. B

3. A

4. A

5. B

6. B

7. B

8. B

9. A

10. A

11. A

12. A

13. A

14. C

15. A

Chapter 6

1. A

2. C

3. A

4. A

5. A

6. A

7. A

8. B

9. A

10. A

Chapter Review Answers

Chapter 1

1. A
2. C
3. C
4. C
5. B
6. A
7. Both A and C
8. B

Chapter 2

1. B
2. A
3. B
4. A
5. B
6. A
7. A

Chapter 3

1. B
2. B
3. B
4. B
5. Both B and C
6. B

Chapter 4

1. A
2. A
3. B
4. B
5. A
6. C

Chapter 5

1. A
2. B
3. C
4. B
5. B

Chapter 6

1. A
2. B
3. A, B, and C
4. B
5. A, B, and C

Recommended Reading and Assumed Platform Knowledge

The VCAP5-DCD blueprint assumes general datacenter knowledge that may be combined with VMware technology in exam questions. If you are a working IT professional with a few years' experience in datacenters and associated installations, this should not be a daunting exam; however, if you are a VMware specialist who rarely ventures outside anything that doesn't begin with a lowercase v, I advise that you spend some time reviewing the basics.

This appendix is split into three sections:

- **Section 1: VMware Recommended Reading List:** This section presents a selection of recommended resources for VMware best practices. Before attempting the VCAP5-DCD exam, make sure you understand the significance of these best practices and use cases for them.

- **Section 2: Assumed Platform Knowledge:** The VCAP5-DCD exam assumes that you have some experience using datacenter technologies. This section includes several tables that provide the kind of information that a seasoned architect should have in his or her head.

- **Section 3: vSphere Design Choice Thoughts:** To succeed at the VCAP5-DCD exam and to create good real-life designs, you need to develop an effective questioning strategy. This section presents the design choice diagrams from earlier chapters—all in one place. Use them to create questions and ensure that you have covered all areas of good design while reviewing best practices.

Section 1: VMware Recommended Reading List

A hyperlinked version of this reading list is available on my website, www.elasticsky.co.uk/dcdguide:

- Design Best Practices for VMware ThinApp (The overview of design is excellent. Note that the technical content is not aimed at the VCAP5-DCD exam.)

- VMware vCloud Implementation Example white paper (This is a great example of a high-level design.)

- VMware vSphere 5.0 Availability Guide

- VMware vSphere High Availability 5.0 Deployment Best Practices

- Performance Best Practices for VMware vSphere 5.0

- VMware vSphere vMotion Architecture, Performance and Best Practices in VMware vSphere 5

- VMware vSphere 5.0 Upgrade Best Practices

- Installing vCenter Server 5.0 Best Practices (VMware KB: 2003790)

- Best Practices for Installing ESXi 5.0 (VMware KB: 2005099)

- vSphere Networking Guide (see page 77)

- Performance Study of VSA in VMware vSphere 5

- Best Practices for vSphere Storage Appliance (VSA) Networking (VMware KB: 2007363)

- Storage I/O Enhancements in vSphere 5.0

- Tuning ESX/ESXi for Better Storage Performance by Modifying the Maximum I/O Block Size (VMware KB: 1003469)

- Understanding Memory Management in VMware vSphere 5

- Best Practices for Performance Tuning of Latency-Sensitive Workloads in vSphere VMs

- Impact of Virtual Machine Memory and CPU Resource Limits (VMware KB: 1033115)

- Setup for Failover Clustering and Microsoft Cluster Service

- Microsoft Clustering on VMware vSphere: Guidelines for Supported Configurations (VMware KB: 1037959)

- Best Practices for vSphere Storage Appliance (VSA) Networking (VMware KB: 2007363)

- Verifying Correct Storage Settings on ESX 4.x, ESXi 4.x and ESXi 5.0 (VMware KB: 1020100)

- Best Practices When Using Advanced Transport for Backup and Restore (VMware KB: 1035096)

- Poor Network Performance or High Network Latency on Windows Virtual Machines (VMware KB:2008925)

- Using Thin Provisioned Disks with Virtual Machines (VMware KB: 1005418)

- Testing Virtual Machine Storage I/O Performance (VMware KB: 1006821)

Section 2: Assumed Platform Knowledge

Table B-1   Raid Levels

Raid Level	Name	Description
0	Striping	Data written to more than one disk at the same time. Increased performance but no redundancy.
1	Mirroring	Redundancy: complete copy on another disk, which means there is no reduction in performance if a disk fails.
5	Striping with parity	Combines performance increases of striping with some redundancy as data can be re-created if a disk fails. Possible performance degradation on disk failure.
1+0	Striping and mirroring	Increased costs due to extra disk requirements. Enables multiple disks to be written to, and there is no performance degradation in the event of a failed disk.

Table B-2   Backup Routines

Routine Name	Description
Full	Copy all files and reset the archive bit
Copy	Copy all files and do not reset the archive bit
Daily	Copy data that changed that day and do not reset the archive bit

Routine Name	Description
Incremental	Copy all data changed since the last full or incremental backup and reset the archive bit
Differential	Copy all data changed since the last full backup and do not reset the archive bit
Transactional	Normally log based (for example, database transaction logs); copy data changed since the last transaction log. Used to recover a system to a specific time. For example, in the event of corruption, restore the last full backup to 3 a.m. and replay transactions to 5 minutes before corruption occurred.

Table B-3   Commonly Used Port Numbers

Port	Function
80	HTTP
443	HTTPS
8080	Web Proxy
21	FTP
23	Telnet
25	SMTP (email)
53	DNS
110	POP3
1433	SQL
1522	Oracle
3260	iSCSI
Port 111/2049	NFS
123 (UDP)	NTP
Standard Custom Range	49000–54000

Table B-4   Basic VMware Port Numbers

Ports Used	Function
80, 443 (TCP)	vSphere client to ESXI host
443 (TCP)	vSphere client to vCenter
902 (TCP/UDP)	vCenter to hosts communication
903 (TCP)	Virtual machine remote console
9443 (TCP)	vSphere web client GUI
8080 (TCP)	vCenter web management services
8443 (TCP)	vCenter web management services
In: 8042-8045 (TCP/UDP) Out: 2050-2250 (TCP/UDP)	HA agents

Table B-4 is not a comprehensive list, but shows some useful ports for walkthroughs/whiteboarding and troubleshooting with vSphere operations/designs. For a more complete list, refer to the vSphere 5 firewall diagram at www.vreference.com/firewall-diagram/.

Table B-5   Cable and Connections

Specification Cable	Length of Runs
CAT 5	100 meters (328 feet)
CAT 6	100 meters (328 feet)
FCoE	Shorter runs (for example, virtual machine remote console, around 10 meters [32.8 feet])

Note that the main difference between CAT 5 and CAT 6 is bandwidth and transmission performance via the same length of cable.

Section 3: vSphere Design Choice Thoughts

Figure B-1   The Infrastructure Qualities—A Checklist of Thought for General Design

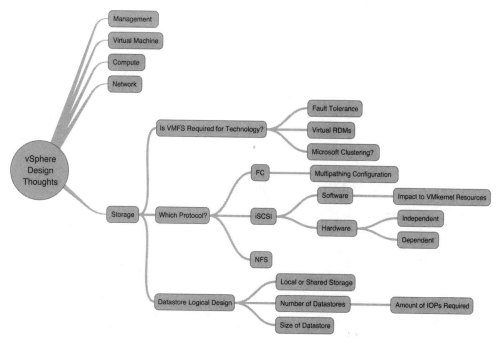

Figure B-2   vThoughts for vSphere Storage Design

Figure B-3   vThoughts for vSphere Network Design

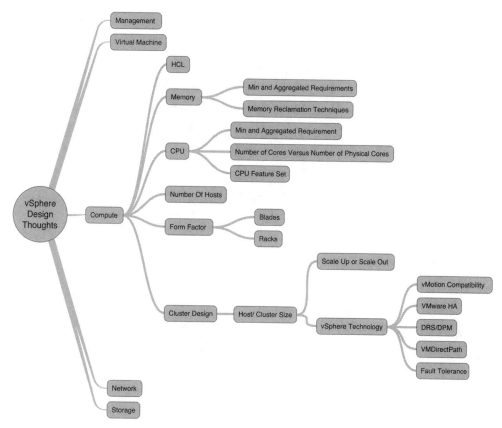

Figure B-4   vThoughts for vSphere Compute Design

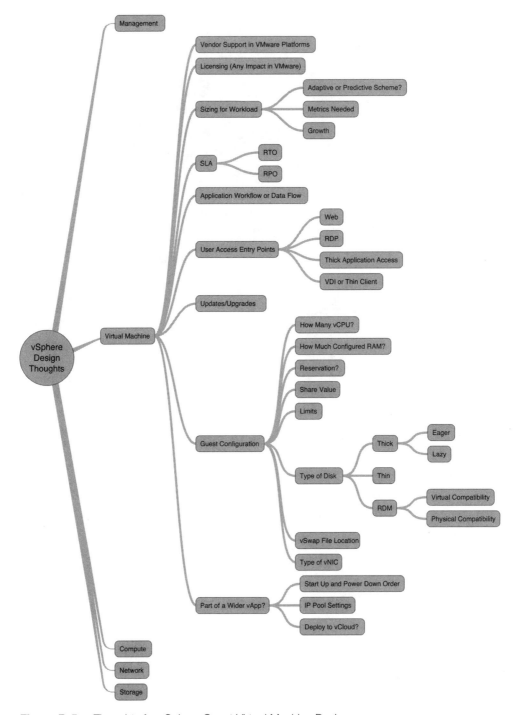

Figure B-5 vThoughts for vSphere Guest Virtual Machine Design

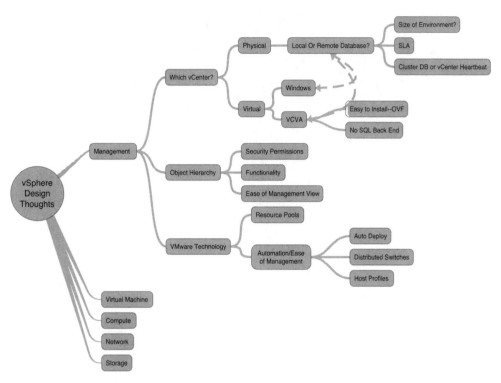

Figure B-6   vThoughts for vSphere Management Design

Glossary

Chapter 1

Assumption A project item that, from the design perspective, is taken to be true without any evidence that it is.

Constraint An item or a situation that can limit a design choice.

Requirement An item that is to be specifically delivered at the end of a project.

Risk An item or a situation that could prevent a project from being completed and the vision from being achieved.

Vision The reason or purpose of starting a project. It is the endpoint or what is required to be created at the end of the project.

Chapter 2

Current state analysis A review of a platform or the items in scope at the beginning of a project, used to establish the starting point of the project environment.

Downstream relationship A logical object or component that does not have a dependency on other items in the solution. For example, say that a multisite web server crashes. The web tier hosting multiple websites will crash; however, the downstream objects such as the database server will continue to function. Backend processes that are dependent on the downstream objects from the web servers can continue to function.

Functional requirement A definable and measurable project item that describes the purpose of a component (that is, its function). An example is "The vSphere platform will host all production workloads with a maximum CPU utilization of 75%."

Gap state analysis A review of the items or tasks required to progress from the current environment to the vision.

Upstream relationship   A logical object or component that has a dependency on other items in the solution. For example, a service running on an application server requires an Active Directory user account to be authenticated. The application service must be started after the Active Directory service. Therefore, the application server has an upstream relationship with the Active Directory service.

Chapter 3

Capacity plan   A report of historical and predictive usage that shows the amount of a resource consumed over time.

Mean time between failures (MTBF)   The anticipated amount of time until a solution component will fail.

Recovery point objective (RPO)   The point in time to which a system needs to be restored following a failure.

Recovery time objective (RTO)   The amount of time it takes to restore a service after a failure takes place.

Service Asset and Configuration Management (CMDB) system   A tool or system that stores the logical services, assets, and configuration components or changes of an IT function or platform.

Chapter 4

Compute layer   The configuration of physical CPU and memory to provide abstracted resources for guest virtual machines.

Network throughput   The amount of traffic (normally in packets) traveling through a system in a given time (for example, seconds) using an available uplink.

Physical design   A guide that illustrates how system components are connected, with sufficient information for real-world implementation. This may include vendor models, IP addresses, and configuration settings.

Storage IOPS   The number of input and output operations per second.

Chapter 5

CPU Ready   The amount of time it takes for a virtual machine to obtain CPU scheduling resources. The larger the CPU Ready value, the longer the virtual machine is not completing its function (for example, the VM is waiting in a queue).

OVF (Open Virtualization Format)   A file format standard that allows the transfer of configured virtual machines.

vApp   An object within vCenter that relates a collection of guest virtual machines. When you add relationships between the guest virtual machines, items such as startup and power on order can be controlled without scripting.

Chapter 6

Entry criteria   The state a platform or component should be in at the start of the current phase. (For example, all ESXi hosts must be of the same build level before guest virtual machines are deployed and validated.)

Exit criteria   The state the platform or component should be in at the end of a task or phase. This should include successful task validation.

Implementation plan   A set of instructions or processes that provide sufficient detail for an engineer to configure or install a platform according to a logical and physical design.

Validation plan   A set of processes to prove that a project or a function of a platform has been configured correctly and behaves as designed.

Index

H

HA (high availability), 41-45

importance of, 90-93

management, 77

heartbeat mechanisms, 109

help desks, 46

high-level design documents. *See* HLDs

HLDs (high-level design documents), 10

Host Profiles, 138

hosts

design, 82

sizing, 83-85

hyperthreading, 115

hypervisors, 38

I

identifiers, GUIDs (globally unique identifiers), 44

impact of changes, 47

implementation, 8, 124

documents, 10

logical design, 62

order of, 27, 127

planning, 137

project execution, 127-128

information gathering, 8, 22-25

implementation, 127

presentation of, 26-29

infrastructure qualities, 38, 41, 60-61

input/output operations per second. *See* IOPS

installation

guides, 137-138

VMs, 108-110

integration, 11, 42

Internet Protocol. *See* IP

interviews

designers, 26

stakeholders, 27

summaries of requirements, 27

invoking disaster recovery, 45

IOPS (input/output operations per second), 69, 72

IP (Internet Protocol) storage, 77

L

latency, 75

lazy-zeroed virtual disks, 113

licensing servers, 133

life cycles of storage platforms, 66

limits of VM guest components, 111

listener services, 42

local storage with vSphere, 65

logging, FT (fault tolerance), 77

logical design

implementation, 62

networks, 78-81

physical design, 81-82

storage, 64

M

management, 11, 38, 60

change, 47

design, 85-90

HA (high availability), 77

layers (vSphere), 63

memory, 109

processes, 8

managers

application, 27

informIT.com THE TRUSTED TECHNOLOGY LEARNING SOURCE

PEARSON **InformIT**

Addison-Wesley | Cisco Press | EXAM/CRAM | IBM Press | QUE | PRENTICE HALL | SAMS | Safari Books Online

LearnIT at InformIT

Looking for a book, eBook, or training video on a new technology? Seeking timely and relevant information and tutorials? Looking for expert opinions, advice, and tips? **InformIT has the solution.**

- Learn about new releases and special promotions by subscribing to a wide variety of newsletters. Visit **informit.com/newsletters**.
- Access FREE podcasts from experts at **informit.com/podcasts**.
- Read the latest author articles and sample chapters at **informit.com/articles**.
- Access thousands of books and videos in the Safari Books Online digital library at **safari.informit.com**.
- Get tips from expert blogs at **informit.com/blogs**.

Visit **informit.com/learn** to discover all the ways you can access the hottest technology content.

Are You Part of the IT Crowd?

Connect with Pearson authors and editors via RSS feeds, Facebook, Twitter, YouTube, and more! Visit **informit.com/socialconnect**.

informIT.com THE TRUSTED TECHNOLOGY LEARNING SOURCE PEARSON

Addison-Wesley | Cisco Press | EXAM/CRAM | IBM Press | QUE | PRENTICE HALL | SAMS | Safari Books Online

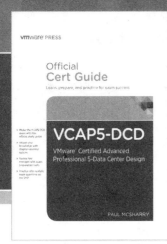

FREE
Online Edition

Your purchase of **VCAP5-DCD Official Cert Guide (with DVD)** includes access to a free online edition for 45 days through the **Safari Books Online** subscription service. Nearly every VMware Press book is available online through **Safari Books Online**, along with thousands of books and videos from publishers such as Addison-Wesley Professional, Cisco Press, Exam Cram, IBM Press, O'Reilly Media, Prentice Hall, Que, Sams.

Safari Books Online is a digital library providing searchable, on-demand access to thousands of technology, digital media, and professional development books and videos from leading publishers. With one monthly or yearly subscription price, you get unlimited access to learning tools and information on topics including mobile app and software development, tips and tricks on using your favorite gadgets, networking, project management, graphic design, and much more.

Activate your FREE Online Edition at
informit.com/safarifree

STEP 1:   Enter the coupon code: QXLAOVH.

STEP 2:   New Safari users, complete the brief registration form.
Safari subscribers, just log in.

If you have difficulty registering on Safari or accessing the online edition,
please e-mail customer-service@safaribooksonline.com